New York City
FIRE TRUCKS

**Wayne Sorenson
& Donald F. Wood**

Published by

**krause
publications**

700 East State Street • Iola, WI 54990-0001
715/445-2214 • FAX: 715/445-4087   www.krause.com

Please call or write for our free catalog of publications. Our toll-free number to place an order or obtain a free catalog is 800-258-0929 or please use our regular business telephone 715-445-2214.

Library of Congress Catalog Number: 2002105755
ISBN: 0-87349-482-2
Printed in the United States of America

Dedicated to
firefighters everywhere

Contents

Preface

Several people generously support a fund at San Francisco State University that supports old truck research. We acknowledge some of the donors: Edward C. Couderc, of Sausalito Moving & Storage, Bev Davis, Jim and Betty Fritts, Gilbert Hall, Bill Hendrickson, David Kiely of ROADSHOW, David Merritt, James Oates, Gene Olson, Oshkosh Truck Foundation, Alvin Shaw, Donald Siegfried, Ray Splinter, Erol S Tuzcu, Ray Unsworth, Art Van Aken, W. T. Van Hook, Charlie Wacker, John E. Waddell, Bill West, Fred Woods, and Daniel Wright.

For preparing this specific book, we acknowledge the help of Dick Adelman, Adam Alberti, Charles Beckwith, Frank J. Fenning, Mollie Fischer, Tim Jackson, Gus Johnson, Garry Kadzielawski, Dan C. Martin, Erin McMahon, Rollie Myers, Joseph Pinto, Reading Body Works, Inc., John Robrecht, Brett Romberg, Lynn Sams, and Warren Weiss. At Krause Publications, we would like to thank Don Gulbrandsen and Brian Earnest.

Wayne Sorensen

Donald F. Wood

Introduction

This is the fourth fire apparatus book that we have co-authored for Krause Publications. In 1993 *American Volunteer Fire Trucks*, was published. We then wrote a two-volume set, with *Big City Fire Trucks, Volume I 1900-1950* being published in 1996, and *Big City Fire Trucks, Volume II 1951-1996* following in 1997. In this book we concentrate solely on the fire apparatus used in New York City by its fire department, widely known as FDNY. Also included are a few photos of equipment operated by other, related New York area agencies.

There is great interest in FDNY these days because of the tragic events of September 11, 2001, that killed many innocent people. At least 10 percent of those who perished were firefighters and police officers involved in rescue operations in the two stricken towers. FDNY — already the subject of other books — is worthy of book coverage for several reasons. The first is its size. New York is our country's largest city with many people and buildings that require protection. Many of the buildings are very tall, which is not the case with buildings in many medium and small U.S. cities. Many of New York's buildings are so tall that a fire can easily be beyond the reach of aerial ladder trucks and fires have to be fought from the inside. The towers in the World Trade Center are the most glaring and tragic example.

Fire apparatus used by FDNY is, and has been, the largest in use anywhere in the U.S. The size of the department also made it possible to run some very specialized, almost one-of-a-kind units that smaller departments could not justify. FDNY has an array of technical support vehicles, such as decontamination units and collapse rescue units. FDNY also buys apparatus in batches, with a typical order containing between two and 20 units.

New York also has a long firefighting history. One can trace the fire service back several centuries and see how the equipment evolved from being pulled and manned by hand, to horse-drawn steam pumpers, to motorized apparatus. New York City also possesses a glamour and attraction and, by many measures, is America's "first" city. FDNY is a proud organization, and is also a source of pride to New York, and to the nation. Firefighters from throughout the U.S. and elsewhere in the world have often held New York City's firefighters in a special high regard due to both the toughness of their assignment and their abilities to carry it out.

Many people think of New York City as being Manhattan, but it consists of five boroughs: Bronx, Brooklyn, Manhattan, Queens, and Staten Island. FDNY operates in all five boroughs. Many of the companies called to the World Trade Center (WTC) were from outside Manhattan. The apparatus shown in the following pages are from all over the city and there are a few pieces shown that are not operated by FDNY.

Chapter 1

The 19th Century and Before

The first settlers in New Amsterdam arrived in about 1625. In 1647, several houses were destroyed by fire and, in 1648, Gov. Peter Stuyvesant issued a proclamation forming a volunteer fire department. In the 1650s, the community's aldermen levied a tax on each household so that 150 leather buckets could be purchased. One third were kept at city hall, the remainder in individual residences. Citizens were expected to leave filled water buckets at their doorstep each night. If the fire alarm sounded they were to grab these filled buckets and run to the site of the fire.

The first two fire apparatus used in New York City arrived by ship from England in 1731. Each pump was to be towed by 20 men and consisted of a large oblong box bound with brass. Inside the box was a condenser case from which a nozzle protruded. Covering the entire top was a large treadle

This circa-1850 Philadelphia-style hand pumper was built by John Agnew of Philadelphia. Both intakes and outlets are visible in the center of the body.

This United States postage stamp, issued in 1948, commemorated the 300th anniversary of Peter Stuyvesant's proclamation forming the nation's first volunteer department.

"which resembled nothing so much as a child's gigantic seesaw, on which 12 men were supposed to perch themselves, clinging to a center handrail and playing 'teeter-totter' in order to furnish motive power for the mechanism."[1] Supplied with each engine were 22 leather buckets to be used to fill the engine's reservoir. In 1737, the colonial General Assembly established the New York Volunteer Fire Department. During this decade New York City consisted of about 9,000 people living in about 1,200 structures on the tip of Manhattan Island.

In 1743 a third engine was added, this one built by a New York coppersmith, Thomas Lote. This engine had no treadles, but was powered by handlebars. Engine four was added in 1749. More engines were added and, in 1772, the first hook and ladder wagon was acquired. By the time of the start of the Revolutionary War, there were eight engine companies and two hook and ladder companies. During the Revolutionary War, many of the volunteers joined Gen. George Washington, and British soldiers occupied New York City in September 1776. Later that year, and again in 1778, major conflagrations destroyed several city blocks.

One of the major steps forward in firefighting can apparently be traced to nearby Philadelphia where, in 1808, a firm began manufacturing riveted leather hose. Up to that time, leather hose had been stitched and the seams could not withstand water pressure. The "substitution of copper rivets for sewn seams finally made leather hose watertight and enabled the firemen to invade buildings in search of flames … {and} the good hose also enabled the volunteers companies to adopt a change in tactics that gradually came into effect, by which they would yoke one engine to another, pumping a continuous stream of water from a river or cistern through a whole cycle of engines to the scene of the blaze, each machine filling another's reservoir and being refilled by another in turn."[2] In the 1820s, hand-drawn hose carts came into use. Volunteer firefighters were exempted from jury and military duty.

In 1839 the Fire Patrol was organized. It was sponsored by insurance companies and its assignment was to protect the contents of commercial buildings from smoke and water damage.

The TV coverage of FDNY since 9/11 shows a sense of brotherhood at each FDNY station and throughout the department. That camaraderie dates back to the days of volunteers. A recent story about "Boss" Tweed, a powerful New York City political boss in the post-Civil War era, said that as a young man, Tweed "became a leader of the local volunteer fire company … {and} he enjoyed the rowdy bonho-

1. Lowell M. Limpas, *History of the New York Fire Department* (New York: E. P. Dutton, 1940), pp. 22-23.
2. Limpas, page 117.

One of two Lee and Larned rotary steam pumpers purchased by New York in 1859. This one was Reading Hose Co. No. 1.

mie of the fire house … {and} what excited Tweed most was beating rival fire companies to the scene of the fire. Running beside his mates as they pulled their fire wagon, he would blow a trumpet and shout."[3] Tweed used his fire company experiences and connections to catapult himself into major positions of political power. Seven New York City mayors could boast of belonging to volunteer fire companies. It must also be conceded that the camaraderie within each volunteer company also extended to engaging in drunken brawls with members of other engine companies.

The steam engine was developed in the early 19th century and one of its potential uses was for fighting fires. In 1855, New York City tested a steam fire engine. The test compared the abilities of the steam engine and a hand pumper. The hand pumper won but, as the test ended, it was also obvious that the hand crew was exhausted while the steam pumper could go on and on.

Steam engines were heavy and needed to be pulled by horses. So the move to steam engines in the 1850s and 1860s signaled a move toward horse-drawn apparatus, and horses also began being used to pull hose carts and hook and ladders. The nature of fire stations changed since they had to accommodate horses and the individual pieces of

apparatus were much larger. Horses required fulltime care. The volunteer system gave way to stations manned by paid, fulltime fire-fighters. Telegraph wires were installed between all of New York's firehouses in 1851.

The shape of steam engines made it difficult for them to carry either hose or personnel, so steam pumpers would be accompanied by a horse-drawn hose company. From then on in New York and other major cities, in the days of horse-drawn apparatus and well into the 20th century when departments were motorized, engine companies would consist of two vehicles — the pumper and the hose wagon. As small chemical (soda/acid) tanks were developed, they were often placed on hose wagons where they would be used for fighting small blazes or attacking large fires until the pumper could get connected to the hydrant and begin pumping water.

In 1880, New York City's department acquired its first water tower. At about this same time, scaling ladders came into use and building inspections were conducted.

At the end of the century, "greater" New York City was formed, embracing an area of more than 300 square miles. The fire department absorbed equipment, personnel, and responsibilities for a much larger area.

3. Kandell, Jonathan, "Boss," *Smithsonian*, February, 2002, page 86.

Engine 33 used this 1865 Amoskeag hose tender that was pulled by a single horse.

Steam-powered railroad locomotives and farm tractors were common in the late 19th century and there were a few attempts to develop steam-driven wagons similar to today's trucks. Commercially the trucks were unsuccessful, mainly because few existing bridges could withstand their weight. This Amoskeag steamer was a demonstrator built in 1868. The steam engine could both propel the vehicle and pump water. It was acquired by FDNY in 1872.

This is FDNY's Amoskeag steam-driven pumper moving through a crowd. Two men are needed to control the steering wheel.

Gleason & Bailey built this four-wheel hose reel with a two-horse hitch. It was used by Engine 14.

The Gleason and Bailey hose wagons had a two-horse hitch. This one is shown in front of Engine 55's station.

Brooklyn apparatus was painted two-tone green. Engine 14 in Brooklyn operated this 1869 Amoskeag second size, 700-gallon per-minute (gpm) steam pumper. (Steam pumpers were classified by size or class. Roughly, a sixth size could pump 300 gpm; fifth size, 400 gpm; fourth size, 500 gpm; third size, 600 gpm; second size, 700 gpm; first size, 800 gpm; extra first size, 900 gpm; and double extra first size, 1000 gpm.)

John Hogan and Abner Greenleaf of Baltimore, Ohio, built this water tower with a 50-foot mast that was pulled by two horses and was raised manually. It was sold to New York City and became Water Tower 1.

This is a LaFrance steam fire engine from 1895, with a two-horse hitch. It was one of two purchased and used first as Engine Company 4 in Long Island, then as Engine 262.

This is a Gleason & Bailey with a Dederick 85-foot aerial ladder. The truck has a three-horse hitch and a tillerman. Note life net on side.

In 1890, FDNY purchased eight of these Gleason and Bailey hose wagons.

Engine 16 was this horse-drawn LaFrance steam pumper.

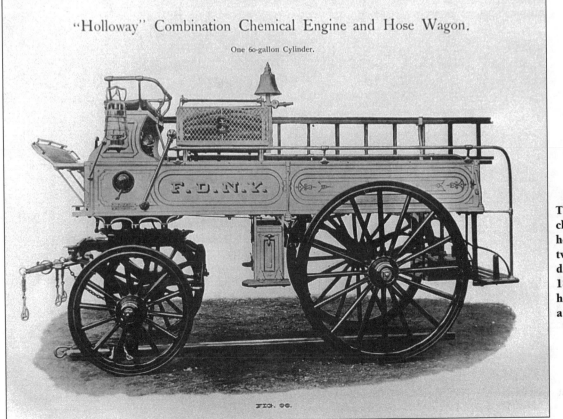

"Holloway" Combination Chemical Engine and Hose Wagon.

One 60-gallon Cylinder.

F.D.N.Y.

FIG. 96.

This Holloway chemical engine and hose wagon had a two-horse hitch. It dated from about 1896. The chemical hose was carried in a basket.

This is one of two 1898 Gleason & Bailey city service trucks that FDNY operated. This one was pulled by two horses and had a tillerman. Note the gong under the floor board, and firemen on running boards. Fire apparatus historian John A. Calderone believes that the term "running board" came from this usage, allowing firemen to use them to "run" to a fire, which they had to do on foot in the era before horse-drawn apparatus.

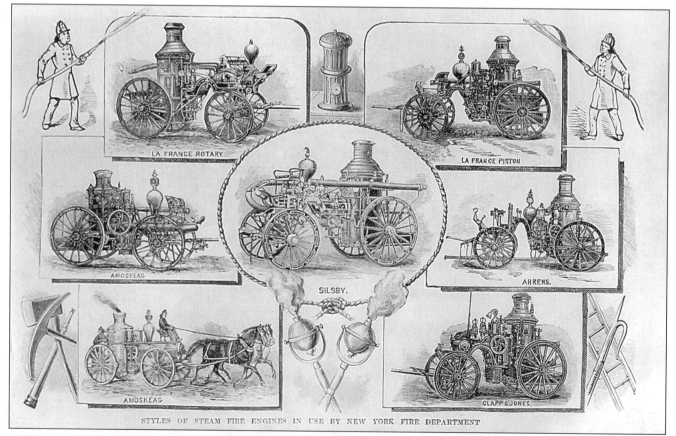

STYLES OF STEAM FIRE ENGINES IN USE BY NEW YORK FIRE DEPARTMENT

These were steam engines used by New York City's Fire Department at the end of the 19th century. They include engines built by Ahrens, Amoskeag, Clapp & Jones, LaFrance, and Silsby.

This 1898 Holloway chemical engine had two chemical cylinders so the operator could work indefinitely as long as the operator had a supply of water, soda, and acid. The apparatus has a two-horse hitch and a platform in the rear on which other firemen could ride. A two-cylinder unit could be recharging one while the other was working.

A horse-drawn LaFrance flood light unit from 1900. A fourth size single-cylinder steam engine powered a Bullock 5 KW generator that, in turn, powered two demountable flood lights. The rig carried 400 feet of electric cable. It was one of three in service.

A flood light truck working at a fire scene.

Chapter 2

1901-1910

Compared with other American cities, New York City has many old buildings and many tall buildings. New York fire historian Gus Johnson used the phrase "Hell's Hundred Acres" to describe an area bounded by Chambers Street, the Bowery, West Broadway and West 8th Street. It was so named because of the great number of firemen who were killed or injured fighting fires in the area. Johnson said that part of the problem was that many of the buildings had suffered numerous fires and the fire damage was repaired superficially, leaving a weakened structure. "Conversion of a tenement to a loft building meant the removal of partitions to provide a large unbroken area for assembly purposes. Try to visualize a large floor area in a garment factory with old-fashioned stoves … and doors that opened inward. Some had no sprinklers; many had boarded-up light courts and no fire escapes. In most of them, finished garments hung on clothes lines above the work benches. Many garment factory fires were started by electric irons left on after closing time."[1]

Wayne Sorensen Collection

This is a steam-powered 1902 Locomobile, FDNY's first motorized vehicle. Chief Croker is shown at the tiller. Next to him is Capt. Robert Oswald. The chief purchased the auto out of his own pocket.

1. Gus Johnson, *F.D.N.Y.* (Belmont, MA: Western Island, 1977), p. 8.

Chemical 12 was this combination chemical and hose wagon, pulled by two horses.

The number of high-rise buildings in the city meant many ladder trucks were needed. However, many buildings towered far above an aerial ladder's reach of 100 feet. So, to reach the fire, the firefighters would often have to go inside the burning structure, attacking the fire from below. Tall buildings have standpipe systems that stretch from the ground to the roof, where there is a water storage tank. At each floor level would be outlets, (where there were connections to stored fire hose). At the bottom, outside the building, were connections through which pumpers could pump additional water into the standpipe system, feeding whatever hoses were in use.

As sprinklers were developed, they would also be linked to the standpipes. Sprinklers are also tied to alarm systems. If heat melts a sprinkler head and water begins flowing, an alarm is activated.

In 1908, a high-pressure water system was installed in downtown Manhattan to increase the flow of water when needed.

According to Lowell Limpas, in 1906 FDNY was manned by 3,562 men who operated 150 engines and 50 hook and ladders. In addition, there were 12 volunteer companies in outlying areas of Staten Island and Queens. In 1906 the department was completely dependent upon horse-drawn apparatus. In 1904, it had acquired two Mercedes automobiles and, in 1906, a Simplex and two Bakers. Its other 1906 acquisitions were horse-drawn and included 13 steam fire engines, five 85-foot aerial ladder trucks, seven 75-foot aerial ladder trucks, one horse ambulance, 15 hose wagons, 10 chief's buggies and one coffee van.[2]

In 1910, FDNY began acquiring gasoline-powered apparatus, including a gasoline-driven pump on a horse-drawn wagon. Some of the earliest deliveries of gasoline apparatus proved to be unsatisfactory. This would probably be the peak of the department's use of horses. In 1910, 918 horses were assigned to engine companies, 287 to ladder companies, 73 to battalion chiefs, 17 to deputy chiefs, 12 to water towers, 10 to boat tenders, and 282 for miscellaneous duties and in reserve.[3]

2. Johnson, p. 55.
3. Johnson, p. 65.

A 1904 American LaFrance, second size, 700-gpm steam-powered pumper inside a New York firehouse. In the center of picture is the station's brass pole. At left are the raised harnesses under which the team will be backed. At far left is the alarm box. This was a time before telephones were widely used. The fire department maintained alarm boxes at most street intersections, in major buildings, and inside each firehouse. In the field, an officer wishing to communicate with headquarters, say, to turn in a second alarm, would use an alarm box on a nearby corner.

Backing horses into a two-horse hitch in front of a 1904 American LaFrance, second size steam pumper. Note firemen on poles.

Hook and Ladder Co. 28 was a 1908 Seagrave 75-foot aerial ladder that was raised by a spring hoist. Ladder crews needed many large men because of the strength required to raise ground ladders. There are three matched white horses in front, and a tillerman riding at the rear.

Waterous Engine Works built this 1905, 300-gpm sixth class gasoline-powered pump. It was used as Engine 1.

A horse-drawn water tower with water being discharged from its deck gun.

In 1910 a Westinghouse 500-gpm pumper driven by a four-cylinder, four-cycle gasoline engine, used by Engine 106 on an experimental basis. It was mounted on a horse-drawn chassis. Note the suction hose and suction strainer.

Gus Johnson photo

This is a tillered American LaFrance 65-foot aerial ladder used by FDNY. It has a three-horse hitch. Under the front floorboard is a large gong that was sounded by stomping on a foot pedal.

This is an ornately trimmed 1910 Knox with a 500-gpm pump undergoing pump tests for FDNY. It failed the tests and was rejected.

Firemen's Day at Union Square in 1910. The truck in the middle is Ladder 3, an American LaFrance 65-foot aerial, pulled by three horses.

The Combination Ladder Co., of Providence, Rhode Island, built this chemical and hose car. It carried two 35-gallon Holloway chemical tanks and 200 feet of 1 1/4-inch chemical hose.

Here the chemical and hose car is carrying six firefighters. The engine was rated at 40 hp and the rig could travel at 40 mph!

Chapter 3

1911-1920

On March 25, 1911, New York's most tragic fire of the 20th century took place in a 10-story building housing the Triangle Shirtwaist Co., which employed 600 immigrant women. It's believed that 146 were killed in the blaze. The fire brought about changes in fire codes and their enforcement, and brought attention to the severe and hazardous conditions under which many immigrants toiled. The anniversary of this tragedy is still marked each year with a small program.

At the beginning of the 1910s, FDNY dabbled in motorized apparatus acquisitions, then moved decisively. In 1911 it bought Ford Model Ts for its deputy chiefs and by 1913 FDNY had made its last purchase of horses. By 1915 the department was considered to be half-motorized. In 1915, FDNY bought 92 pieces of motorized apparatus. In that same year, masks were provided to the first FDNY rescue company, which used in a Cadillac.

Ed Gardner photo

On the right is a 1916 South Bend hose wagon from Engine 38 with a deck pipe. It is one of seven. Left center is a Christie two-wheel tractor pulling a steam pumper. At left is a horse-drawn hose wagon, also with a deck pipe. Note that horses have been moved from the scene.

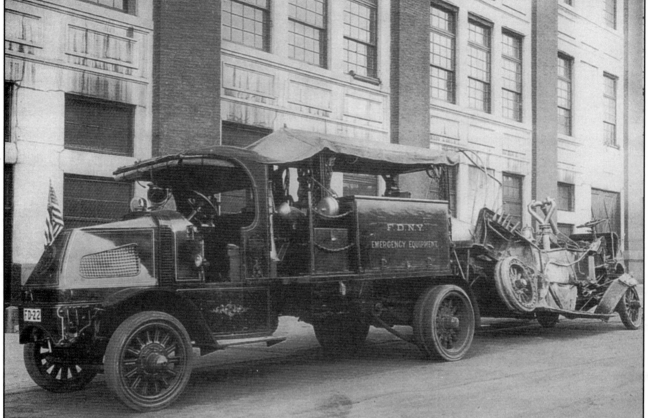

Gus Johnson photo

A 1917 Mack AC "Bulldog" used as a heavy-duty wrecker/recovery vehicle by FDNY is shown pulling the remnants of a 1911 Knox hose wagon that had been crushed by a collapsing wall.

Tenement fires became an issue during this decade. FDNY implemented a program of monthly inspections by uniformed firemen of tenement cellars, hallways, and stairs. Fire prevention was taught in the schools and 1 million copies of a fire prevention booklet were printed and distributed to students. The program's success was judged by a reduction in tenement fires. In 1914, 1915, and 1916, there were 19,204 tenement fires, which was a reduction from the previous three-year period when 21,235 were recorded.[1]

World War I started in Europe in 1914 and in the spring of 1917, the United States declared war on Germany. An article in the May, 1917, issue of *The American City*, New York Fire Commissioner Robert Adamson told how his department was responding to the nation's involvement in war. Some of what he described was not unlike descriptions of response to the WTC tragedy some 84 years later. FDNY's plan included:

— Organizing an auxiliary fireboat fleet consisting of private tugboats. At that time there were 143 tugs in the port area, most belonging to railroads that used them to carry lighters between New Jersey and cargo ships moored in Manhattan. The tugs could pump water and the waterfront was laid

out into zones. When there was a fire alarm, the department dispatcher would notify the railroad to send at least two tugs to the fire site. Tugboat captains were to be given firefighting instruction by FDNY personnel.

— Adding controls on the movement of explosives. Contractors who stored explosives had to maintain two watchmen at night if they wished to keep their blasting permits. (The fear was of German saboteurs.) There were also to be additional controls on movements of dangerous chemicals.

— Authorizing 10 additional fire companies along with funds to staff them, provide them with apparatus, and buy additional hose.

— Forming an auxiliary firefighting force of 1,500-2,000 men. It consisted of retired firefighters still in good health, one-time volunteers in various departments who lived in the area, and those who were on waiting lists for appointments to FDNY. The plan stated: "We have enough men on the volunteer rolls to man practically every fire company in the city, if necessary. In case of a serious emergency, the regular force of firemen will be concentrated in the central part of the city, where the danger is greatest, and the volunteers will be used to man the companies in the outlying districts,

1. "The Results of Fire Prevention Education," *The American City* (February, 1917), pp. 160-161.

This is one of 12 Mack combination chemical and city service trucks. The letters "F.D.N.Y. H. & L. CO." are painted alongside, with the station number yet to be added.

where fires are very few and where the possibility of extensive incendiarism would be remote."

— Postponing vacations and time-off allowances.

— Providing police guards for the fire department headquarters and the two high-pressure pump stations. Wherever the high-pressure "pipes are exposed to subway excavations, police will also be stationed." Other arrangements with the police include response to "riot calls," which will "bring firemen, with their effective hose and high-pressure water service, to the side of the policemen in quelling serious street disorders."

— Completing motorization of the department by buying 45 tractors to pull steamers, 45 tenders, and both city service and aerial ladder trucks.

— Increasing fire prevention campaigns.[2]

The war ended in November, 1918, but there was considerable social unrest and agitation in some European countries and some U. S. cities. In 1919 the Uniformed Firefighters Association was formed in New York City. On September 16, 1920, a horse-drawn wagon loaded with dynamite exploded on Wall Street, in front of the J. P. Morgan offices, killing 44 people.

FDNY used this 1911 Knox, model R5, as a supply wagon.

Wayne Sorensen Collection

2. Robert Adamson, "Emergency Measures Adopted by the New York City Fire Department," The American City, May, 1917, pp. 485-488.

Lynn Sams Collection

A 1912 two-wheel Cross front-drive tractor pulling an 1898 first size Metropolitan steam-powered 800-gpm pump. It ran as Engine 1.

Gus Johnson photo

This 1912 photo, taken in front of Engine 20, shows a mixture of horse- and motor-powered rigs. At left is a Knox-Webb high-pressure hose wagon; then a horse-drawn chief's buggy; a horse-drawn LaFrance steam-powered search light wagon; another horse-drawn chief's buggy, and a motorized 1911 Knox hose wagon with a deck pipe. High-pressure wagons relied on special hydrants that supplied water at higher pressure. It was sufficient to connect hoses to those hydrants without using a pumper.

Dan Martin photo

A 1911 Webb Couple Gear, gas-electric tractor, installed at Water Tower Company 1, replacing three horses. It's attached to Water Tower 1, a 65-foot, hydraulically raised water tower built by the International Fire Engine Co.

STANDARD "WEBB" FOUR-CYLINDER PISTON PUMPING ENGINE

Gus Johnson photo

Webb built this 500-gpm pumper for FDNY in 1911, but it was not accepted after tests.

A 1911 Knox hose wagon follows a 1911 Waterous with 750-gpm pump.

In 1911, FDNY bought 10 Ford Model T runabouts for deputy chiefs. The cars were outfitted at the FDNY shops.

All 10 1911 Ford Model T runabouts were deputy chiefs' cars.

Lynn Sams Collection

This 1911 Waterous, with a 750-gpm piston pumper, was purchased to serve as Engine 39. However, it was not considered to be satisfactory, and was removed from service.

This 1911 Nott was propelled by a gasoline engine, which powered the wheels through a chain drive. The pump was powered by steam and was rated at 700 gpm.

Here we see the Nott in service, although the Notts were eventually withdrawn because their performance was unsatisfactory. On the right note the blanketed horses. At the fire site it was always necessary to care for them.

A 1911 Webb Couple Gear, gas-electric tractor, installed at Water Tower Company 1, replacing three horses. It's attached to Water Tower 1, a 65-foot, hydraulically raised water tower built by the International Fire Engine Co.

Two fire apparatus destroyed by a collapsing wall, circa 1911.

FDNY's first motorized aerials were a set of three, purchased from Webb in 1912. This Webb 75-footer is shown with a full crew.

Engine 117 was this 1912 Webb Couple Gear electric tractor hitched to a 1907 Nott first size (900-gpm) steam pumper. The rig was very slow and considered to be unsatisfactory.

Engine 6, a steam fire engine, frozen at the Equitable Building fire in 1912.

This 1912 Mack-Boyd chemical and hose wagon was shown in a Goodyear tire ad undertaking its hill-climbing test.

Wayne Sorensen Collection

This photo was taken in about 1912 and shows three pieces of apparatus. On the outsides are two 1912 Mack high-pressure hose wagons, with Boyd-built bodies. They had spring-wound starters (behind the front bumper), carried twin chemical tanks, and were known as "Scouts." (The spring-wound starter was wound up tightly when the truck was stopped. A release lever was activated by a cable that reached to the operator's seat. When released, the spring would turn the crank, starting the engine.) Note the dog on the running board of the distant Scout. In the center is Engine 93, an American LaFrance Metropolitan second size steam pumper, pulled by a 1913 Christie tractor.

Here is a front view of the 1912 Mack-Boyd hose wagon. They would accompany a steam-pumper to the fire site. Note the driver is not a uniformed Fireman.

In this 1913 photo we see a 1913 Christie tractor attached to a steam pumper, followed by a Mack-Boyd "Scout" combination chemical and hose wagon.

A circa-1913 Mack hose wagon on a cold winter day.

In a ceremony repeated everywhere, horses were replaced by motorized apparatus, as shown here in front of Engine 230 in 1913. From left we see a 1913 Mack-Boyd combination chemical and hose wagon; a 1913 Christie tractor attached to a steam pumper; and the displaced steam pumper, pulled by three horses.

Ladder 37 was one of 25 aerial ladders that FDNY purchased from American LaFrance in 1913. Seventeen of them were 60-foot aerials, eight were 75 feet.

A 1913 Christie two-wheeled tractor attached to a tillered 1913 Seagrave 85-foot aerial ladder. Note driver has a single seat.

Engine 91 was this American LaFrance steamer pulled by a 1913 Christie tractor. It was one of an order of 28.

A. Hardy photo

Lynn Sams Collection

Engine 160 was this 1913 Nott combination pumper and hose car. It had a 500-gpm rotary gear pump and was one of two purchased.

Engine 37 was a Christie tractor linked to an American LaFrance second-size steam pumping engine.

Wayne Sorensen Collection

This 1914 Cadillac chassis with a modified auto body was placed in service during March of 1915 as Rescue Squad No. 1. It carried oxygen tanks, "oxygen helmets," a pulmotor, rigging equipment, jacks, a cutting torch, life belts and life lines, and assorted first aid equipment. One of its first major calls was to the site of a subway tunnel, under construction, that had collapsed. This was the first rescue company in the United States.

Note that the steering wheel is horizontal on this 1912 Webb Tractor pulling a 900-gpm steam pump. All three of these tractors had different front configurations.

Christie tractors took the place of horses. In 1914, FDNY bought 42 Christie single-axle tractors. Here we see Christie tractors in front of a steam engine and an aerial ladder truck.

This Christie was attached to a steam pump, shown working at a fire. Christie made its last deliveries to FDNY during 1916.

This 1914 two-wheel Christie tractor was linked to a 1906 Seagrave 85-foot aerial ladder. It ran as Ladder 1, stationed on Duane Street.

Two apparatus destroyed as a building collapsed. At left is a 1911 Knox hose wagon that was Wagon No. 2. At right is a 1914 Garford tractor attached to a water tower.

A circa-1914 Locomobile ambulance used by FDNY. FDNY began providing ambulance service for injured firefighters om 1914.

Gus Johnson photo

A church fire in New York City during World War I. At left is a tractor-drawn steam pumper; at right is a Mack hose wagon.

Gus Johnson photo

A circa-1915 White with specialized equipment that FDNY used for thawing frozen hydrants in the winter.

This 1915 Ahrens–Fox Model MK pumper was one of an order of six. It had a six-cylinder engine and riveted fenders. It could pump 700 gpm, and its pump had a single-chamber ball. This was Engine 95. Note that operator sits closer to the rear axle than to the front.

This is Engine 95 working at a fire scene.

A circa-1915 Ford Model T roadster, used at the Deputy Chief level in the FDNY.

Three 1916 South Bend combined chemical and hose wagons. The two in the distance are equipped with deck pipes.

Ed Gardner photo

On the left is Engine 221, a Christie tractor-drawn steam pumper. On the right is a horse-drawn hose wagon with a deck gun. The horses have been unhitched and removed from the site.

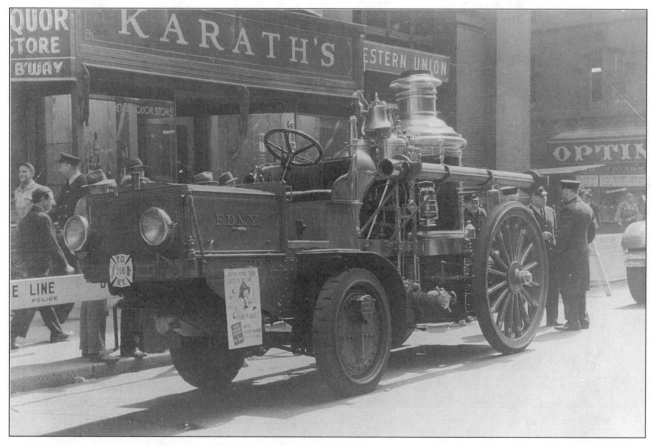

A 1917 Van Bierck front-drive tractor pulling a 1913 American LaFrance second size, 750-gpm steam pumping engine. This was Engine Company 116.

Lynn Sams Collection

In 1917, FDNY took delivery of six of these Robinson combination pump and hose wagons with 700-gpm piston pumps. This one served as Engine 50.

Wayne Sorensen Collection

This is a 1917 American LaFrance Type 75, 700-gpm pumper with a deck gun. It was one of 25.

On the left is a World War I era-American LaFrance pumper pumping water through its deck gun and feeding water to the deck gun on the circa-1913 Mack hose wagon on the right.

A 1918 Garford city service truck that carried ladders and chemical tanks with hose.

Charles Beckwith Collection

Around 1920, Edgewater Camp, in the Borough of the Bronx, was a summer resort community relying on a volunteer fire department for protection. Here is its circa-1920 Ford TT, outfitted by American-LaFrance as a combination chemical and hose car. The sign on fire station in the rear says: "Edgewater Camp Volunteer Hose Co. No. 1," and similar lettering appears on the truck. Note its two large floodlights.

Charles Beckwith Collection

The same Ford is shown participating in a local parade, circa 1940.

Chapter 4

1921-1930

By 1921, FDNY was almost completely motorized and had more than 6,000 men on its roster. They were organized into 306 companies.

Gus Johnson wrote that a new hazard had arisen: exploding stills. Prohibition had started in 1919, which caused many drinkers to make their own spirits. The problem was most distilling processes involved use of fires, and alcohol and fire were not a good mixture.

In the early 1920s, FDNY was operating 11 fireboats through its Marine Division. Most fireboats had very large-capacity pumps and, in addition to sending water on to the fire directly, they would supply lines that were carried inland.

In 1921, FDNY completed motorizing its fleet of ladder trucks and, by about 1923, the department would be completely motorized. The last run by a horse-drawn FDNY vehicle was made by Engine Co. 205 in Brooklyn on December 20, 1922.[1]

Fire apparatus historian Mathew Lee wrote that bids for pumpers required that the fire engine's brakes could hold on a 15-percent grade; that they could turn within 35 degrees, and pump at capacity at no more

Charles Beckwith Collection

Ladder 76 used a city service body built on a 1926 Pierce-Arrow truck chassis. It also carried both ladders and chemical tanks and hose.

1. http://www.nycfiremuseum.org/History/hist11.html December 5, 2001.

than 1100 rpms of the motor. He added that FDNY also specified extra radiators and wheels with each order. Specifications for hose wagons delivered in 1927 included: seat rail must be 4 inches above the seat; rear step not less than 14 inches off the ground; fenders of not less than 14-gauge steel; hose box floor of ash not less than 1 1/8 inch thick; hose box 12 feet long and 22 inches high; Wheaton-type turret pipe; and pipe tips from 1 1/4-to 1 3/4-inch sizes. Lee wrote: "No one could argue with specifications that called for 'the bracketing of ladders that must not allow any sagging of the ladders,' or for 'use only second growth white hickory for pompier ladders.' But, the specs. also indicated a multitude of requirements right down to the handles of the pike poles to be white ash and FDNY to be stamped on the lanterns. These demands seem excessive when other cities' work orders are reviewed."[2]

Lee also wrote: "The decade of the '20s saw many changes in the life of a fireman. In many cities,

horses left fire service during the decade. Although we might view the horse with an air of romanticism, eliminating the horse meant the elimination of a lot of extra work for the firefighter. The firefighter was considered more of a professional and less of an animal tender as horses passed from the scene. In previous decades, group shots of firemen were seldom taken with their apparatus. Firemen of the 1920s knew that the motor apparatus made their jobs easier and enhanced their image."[3]

Private Fire Patrols in New York, sponsored by insurance companies to protect contents of burning structures, reached their peak in 1929, according to Gus Johnson. At that time they operated 20 trucks based in 10 stations and employed 316 men. Johnson wrote "In 1929 each salvage wagon carried 25 covers, also forcible entry tools, two five-gallon extinguishers, a 14-foot Pompier ladder, life belts, a rope life net, shovels, brooms, scoops, and equipment for repairing sprinkler systems."[4] At large fires in Manhattan as

This is one of 12 Seagrave model "L" 75-foot aerials, delivered to FDNY in 1925. It's shown responding to an alarm. The steering wheel is on the left, and a captain in white turn-out gear rides on the other seat.

American Automobile Manufacturers Association

2. Mathew Lee, *A Pictorial History of the fire engine, volume 2, the decade of the 1920s.* (Plymouth, Michigan: the author, 1999), p. 248.
3. Lee, volume 2, p. 422.
4. Johnson, p. 29-30.

many as eight Patrol trucks would respond and hundreds of covers would be spread, mainly to protect inventory from water damage. "More than 900 covers were spread at one piano factory fire, a single piano sometimes requiring two covers."5 (In 1956, William Feehan, New York City's ranking fireman killed on 9/11, began his fire fighting career with the New York Fire Patrol.)

A water tower in operation in the 1920s. In the foreground is an aerial ladder truck

5.   Ibid.

Wayne Sorensen Collection

Engine 274 was this 1921 American LaFrance Type 75 combination pump and hose car. Its pump was rated at 700 gpm. It was one of a batch of 20.

This is one of two American LaFrance 65-foot aerials purchased in 1921.

The fireboat "John Purrey Mitchel," built in 1921, was named after a former mayor.

A well-equipped circa-1921 Mack "Bulldog" city service truck that ran as Hook and Ladder Co. 244. It was one of four ordered at the same time.

Charles E. Beckwith photo

This 1921 Mack AC city service truck was converted in 1942 to an "Emergency Utility Unit."

A 1921 Mack AC tractor pulling a tillered 75-foot aerial ladder. Firefighters are in dress uniforms, posing for the photo.

Gus Johnson photo

Here's a photo for Mack Bulldog fans. A tillered aerial ladder is in the right center. To the left is a water tower in action.

Wayne Sorensen Collection

FDNY's shops converted this 1921 White/Pirsch city service truck to a smoke ejector and foamite unit.

Wayne Sorensen Collection

Here is a 1921 White salvage wagon, with its equipment on display.

John J. Robrecht photo

This 1921 White chassis had a city service/chemical body installed by Pirsch. It was one of 10.

This 1922 American LaFrance was one of an order of 22. Its pump was rated at 700 gpm. The headlight lenses are red.

In 1939, FDNY's shops converted this 1922 American LaFrance 700-gpm pumper to a chemical truck for use on bridges. Note the foam powder hopper behind the rear wheel.

Horses making their last run for FDNY on December 20, 1922.

Gus Johnson photo

This 1922 FWD tank truck was a fuel tender used for carrying gasoline, oil, and water. In the days of steam pumpers, fuel wagons would carry coal. At the time of this photo, the gasoline/oil refuelers carried a surprisingly high proportion of oil since internal combustion engines in that era burned much more oil than modern engines. Today, tenders carry mainly diesel fuel.

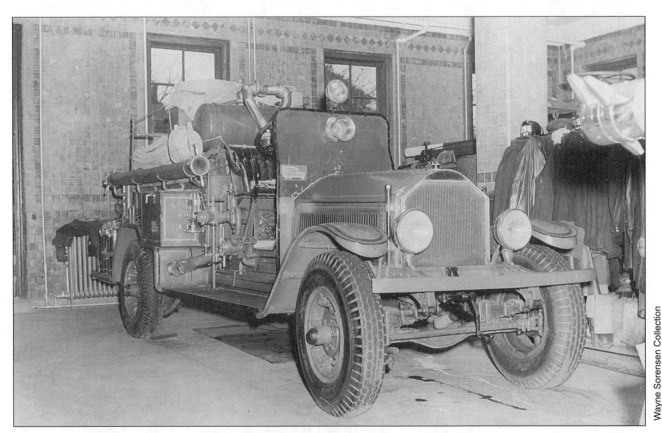

Wayne Sorensen Collection

This is a 1923 American LaFrance Type 75 pumper with a 700-gpm pump. In 1939 it was converted in the FDNY shops into a chemical truck for use on bridges.

Hose wagon 30 was this 1923 Mack with a scaling ladder and a mounted deck gun. Scaling (or pompier) ladders had an elbow at the top. A fireman would use the elbow to break the glass in a window above and, after making certain the ladder was secure, he would climb to the broken window, secure himself, and then repeat the operation, climbing up another story.

This 1924 International pickup was used by FDNY's Bureau of Fire Alarm Telegraph to maintain its electrical alarm system.

Frank J. Fenning

This 1925 Mack AC was originally a rescue squad truck, serving first as Rescue 2, then as Rescue 4. It is shown here after it was converted to a foam and powder supply unit. On the side is a double role of hose and a spare tire.

Charles Beckwith Collection

This 1925 Seagrave 75-foot aerial ran as Ladder 18. Note that headlights are painted over except for small slits. This was probably to function as "black-out" lights during World War II. (The photo was taken in the mid-1940s.)

Wayne Sorensen Collection

Pirsch outfitted this 1927 International to serve as a hose wagon. It came with a mounted deck gun and was one of 12.

This 1,000-gpm 1927 Ahrens-Fox was FDNY's first pumper with pneumatic tires. It ran as Engine 65 and later as Engine 276. This particular engine was pictured in Ahrens-Fox literature, accompanied by this statement that originally ran in the June 3, 1927, issue of *The New York World*: "The question of adequate fire protection for the upper floors of the tall apartment, hotel, and office buildings of New York is believed to be effectively settled with the placing in service tomorrow morning of what Chief Kenlon characterized as 'a lulu' in fire apparatus. Rated at 140 horsepower, weighing 12,000 lbs., 24 feet in length, with a six-cylinder piston pump designed to deliver 1,000 gallons of water a minute under a pressure of 160 lbs. to the square inch at the pump, this engine yesterday exceeded all claims made for it by its makers, the Ahrens-Fox Company."

This 1927 American LaFrance type 119 pumper could pump 1,000 gallons per minute and ran as Engine 237. It was one of six and delivered with solid rubber tires that were later replaced with pneumatics.

This is one of 20 FWD tractors that FDNY bought in 1927. This one was coupled with a 1918 American LaFrance 65-foot aerial, and operated as Ladder 53. Note the solid rubber tires. Mathew Lee quoted one fireman who said this about FWDs: "It took a 200-lb. man to steer 'em and the ride was like that of a bucking bronco … you couldn't tire the damn things out!"

A 1927 FWD tractor pulling a 1904 Femco 65-foot water tower. Note that the outriggers are extended.

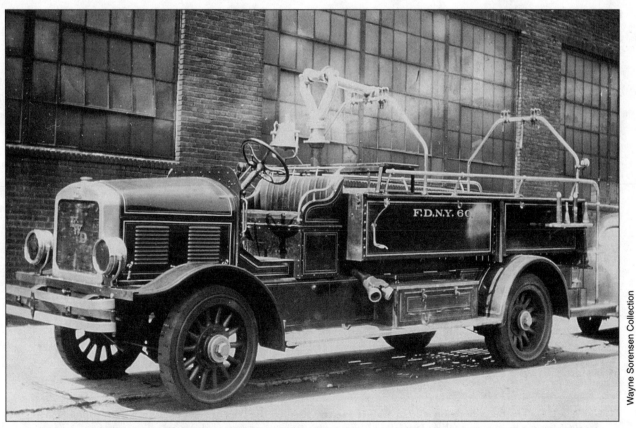

Hose Wagon 60 was this 1928 FWD with bodywork by Pirsch. It was one of 18. Note the mounted deck gun and hand or grab rail around the driver's seat. Headlight lenses are red.

Frank J. Fenning photo

This 1928 FWD/Pirsch hose wagon ran with Engine 263. Note deck gun. Instead of headlights, there appears to be two small red lights.

This is a tunnel recovery body on a 1928 Walker Electric used by the Port of New York Authority. It had nearly identical towing booms on each end and could operate in either direction. It also carried several large chemical tanks for fighting fires.

Lynn Sams Collection

This stylish 1929 Packard open sedan was converted into Searchlight No. 4. It was one of two given to the department as a gift.

John J. Robrecht

This 1930 American LaFrance 65-foot water tower was the last water tower acquired by FDNY. The mast was raised hydraulically and it had two mast nozzles. It ran as Water Tower No. 6. At this late date it still came with curb-side steering solid tires and tiller steering. Note the tiller at the back of the tower.

Here on the 1930 Amercian LaFrance, we see the outriggers extended and mast elevated.

This is one of seven Mack 700-gpm pumpers delivered in 1930 with no windshield and hard rubber tires.

Engine 244, a 1930 Mack, shown fighting a stubborn fire at Coney Island in 1940.

The volunteers at Edgewater Camp used this 1930 Paramount as a small, 300-gallon tanker. Paramounts were taxicabs, built in Hagerstown, Maryland, between 1927 and 1931.

This is the same tanker after a facelift – or possible accident? The radiator and hood come from a later model Paramount and sealed beam units have been installed in the headlights.

Frank J. Fenning photo

This 1930 Mack was first assigned as Engine 267. Soon it became a spare and was photographed in 1934 at a resort area where it was in service on summer weekends only.

Lynn Sams Collection

Walter is a well-known regional truck builder specializing in all-wheel drive chassis. This all-wheel-drive 1930 Walter tractor was coupled with an 1895 Hale 65-foot water tower. It was Water Tower 2.

Chapter 5

1931-1940

On August 1, 1932, eight New York City fire-fighters were killed at a fire at the Ritz Tower. There was a major explosion in a paint storeroom in a sub-basement of the 40-story hotel.

New York's colorful mayor, Fiorello H. LaGuardia, could be spotted on the sidelines at major fire sites. LaGuardia increased spending for fire apparatus, saying: "No personnel of a great department can function without proper tools." In the years 1935, 1936, and 1937, FDNY spent $1.2 million for equipment, over twice the amount spent for 1932, 1933, and 1934. LaGuardia said that the increase in expenditures for equipment was more than offset by reduction in fire losses. In 1933 the loss was $9.7 million; by 1936 it was reduced to $7.7 million.

During this decade, FDNY acquired about 10 thawing units that generated steam for heating frozen hydrants. It also bought two air compressor units for rescue work.

A report by the chief of the Bureau of Fire Alarm Telegraph in early 1937 indicated that the city had 9,817 fire-alarm boxes on street locations, plus 818 in schools. In 1936, 48,180 alarms were transmitted, including 8,560 false alarms. The report said: "Although the telephone is used extensively and is of invaluable aid to the Department, especially in outlying sections where fire-alarm boxes are not closely spaced, we most strongly urge the use of the fire-alarm box for transmitting an alarm of fire. The fire-alarm box is more dependable, less liable to cause mistakes, and insures a more rapid and

Ed Hass photo

Ladder 41 was this 1940 Ahrens-Fox with an 85-foot aerial.

adequate response of fire companies."[1] One of the New Deal's job-creating programs, the Works Progress Administration (WPA), funded employment of men to both string new fire alarm telegraph lines and to maintain existing ones by cutting back surrounding branches.

An article in a 1939 issue of *The American City* gave this inventory of FDNY's organization and equipment: 222 engine companies, 125 hook and ladder companies, four rescue companies and 10 fireboats. FDNY owned over a million feet of hose: 64,000 feet of 1 1/2-inch; 718,000 feet of 2 1/2-inch; 130,000 feet of 3-inch; and 33,000 feet of 3 1/2-inch. Most of the personnel were full-time, although there were still two volunteer hose companies on Staten Island. FDNY's 10 fireboats carried two-way radios and its 12 deputy chief cars carried one-way radios. In the five-year period from 1934-1938, FDNY purchased new 99 pumpers, 48 ladder trucks, 22 hose wagons, two tractors, 13 hydrant service trucks, two searchlight trucks, 91 automobiles, 17 delivery trucks, and one rescue wagon. Of the 30,000 fires that FDNY fought in 1938, only 10 spread outside the building where they had origi-nated. Two-thirds of the fires fought caused less than $10 (in 1938 dollars) damage. By 1939, there were more than 10,500 men in FDNY, and they were organized into 391 companies.

The decade is known best for the Great Depression, with large numbers of Americans unemployed. Toward the decade's end, there were wars in both Europe and Asia. Aerial bombing was having devastating effects on large cities and it was clear that large U.S. cities would be likely targets if the U.S. were to become involved in war. In 1940 several FDNY battalion chiefs were sent to London to observe the destruction caused by German bombing.

Prior to Pearl Harbor, this brief item appeared in an issue of *The American City*: "Fire Commissioner Patrick Walsh estimates that more that 40,000 civilians will soon be trained in New York City as members of the Emergency Fire Auxiliary Corps, a unit of the civil defense program. Most of the instruction periods will be in the evening, so as not to conflict with the regular work of members. For training the auxiliary the city has drawn specifications for 660 new pumpers, and 1,000 retired firemen are available."

One of the 1936 FWD aerials.

John J. Robrecht photo

1. "Fire Alarm Policy and Figures in New York City," *The American City*, April, 1937, page 17.

"This 1931 American LaFrance 700-gpm pumper was one of an order of 21. They were the last rotary-gear pumpers purchased by FDNY. They were delivered with hard rubber tires and no windshields. On this one, Engine 12, the tires have been replaced but the windshield is yet to come."

This is one of two Ahrens-Fox model AHP 1,000-gpm pumpers delivered in 1933. They came with hard rubber tires and later were equipped with pneumatic ones.

Frank. J. Fenning photo

This 1931 Bulldog Mack ran as Rescue No. 2. In 1939 the FDNY shops rebuilt it, adding a roof and canvas side curtains. On this side we see a hopper for foam, a stretcher, and thick hose for the smoke ejector.

Frank. J. Fenning photo

On this view, from the curb side, we see a smoke ejector on the running board and a loudspeaker at the front corner of the cab roof.

This is a 1,000-gpm Seagrave model 72 pumper that ran as Engine 163. It was one of eight in an order.

In 1933, FDNY received five Walter tractors with 75-foot aerial ladders on semi-trailers that had been outfitted by the Combination Ladder Company. Note how the engine of the Walter is carried ahead of the front axle. This was to equalize the truck's weight on both axles, necessary for taking full advantage of its all-wheel traction.

John J. Robrecht photo

This 1933 Walter tractor is shown pulling an older American LaFrance ladder. Note the diameter of the tillerman's wheel is larger than that of the steering wheel in the front cab.

This 1934 Ahrens-Fox 1,000-gpm pumper served as Engine 242. One of four delivered in 1934. The Ahrens-Fox Model NT2 1,000-gpm piston pumper came with pneumatic tires.

This is one of four Ahrens-Fox model NT-2 1,000-gpm piston pumpers delivered to FDNY in 1934. They were delivered with pneumatic tires. The steering wheel was on the right, which made it easier for the operator to align with the curb and hydrant.

In 1934, FDNY purchased two FWD tractors to pull 1928 Mack 75-foot aerial semi-trailers. Note chromed louvers. This was Ladder 127.

Note height of tillerman's seat above ground. Also, rear wheels are turned. This was Ladder 152.

Mack photo

These pictures of 1936 pumpers were featured in Mack literature. They were Type 21 1,000-gpm pumpers.

Mack photo

FDNY ordered 20 of these engines.

This is Salvage Truck 2, operated by the New York City Fire Insurance Patrol. It's on a 1936 White chassis.

Hose wagon 18 was one of six 1936 Walter all-wheel drive trucks. An article in *The American City* described the delivery of the six. "The latest six of the 131 hose and turret trucks now belonging to the New York Fire Department were delivered by the Walter Motor Truck Co early in 1936 … Powered with 150-hp six-cylinder special fire-apparatus motors, these trucks can maintain 45 miles per hour, and they hit 52 mph in the test run of 20 miles through New York City in 50 minutes. The automatic locked differential, which prevents any wheel with less traction that the others from slipping, insures that the apparatus will get to the fire regardless of the ground whether snow, sleet or mud."

Charles E. Beckwith photo

Twelve of these 1936 FWD tractors with 85-foot aerial ladders were purchased. This one is Truck No. 3, backing into the station. Both driver and tillerman are looking rearward.

This is one of two 1937 Ward LaFrance searchlight trucks, this one being "Search Light No. 1." They had 10-kw generators and eight large, mobile lights.

Engine 299 was this 1937 Mack Type 21 with cab and a 1,000-gpm pump. It was heavily laden with equipment and was one of an order of 11. Note subway straps at the rear. Apparatus historian Mathew Lee said that these straps were actually supplied by the same firm that supplied straps to the region's subway system.

Wayne Sorensen Collection

In 1938, FDNY received 20 of these Ahrens-Fox model HT 1,000-gpm pumpers. These pumpers came with cabs, piped deck guns and spare tires. Note the stylish lines of the fenders and the "V" windshield; both efforts to add some streamlined touches to a very classic fire engine.

This is a 500-gpm pumper built by Ahrens-Fox on a 1938 Schacht truck chassis, powered by a Hercules engine. It was one of three and served at the New York World's Fair.

This is another of the three Ahrens-Fox-Schachts purchased for use at the World's Fair. After the fair, the three were converted to hose wagons, this one serving as Engine 163. Note that an overhead ladder rack has been added.

Marine Company 9 operated this fireboat "Firefighter," built in 1938. It was FDNY's first diesel-powered boat. It was designed by the firm of Gibbs and Cox and built at United Shipyards. It had four DeLaval pumps, each capable of pumping 5,000 gpm, for a total capacity of 20,000 gpm. It would remain in service until 1988.

This FWD factory photo shows one of 14 1938 FWD 85-foot aerial ladder trucks placed in service by FDNY. The stabilizing jacks are down.

This is one of 14 FWDs with 85-foot aerial ladders placed into service in 1938. Note that tillerman has a windshield.

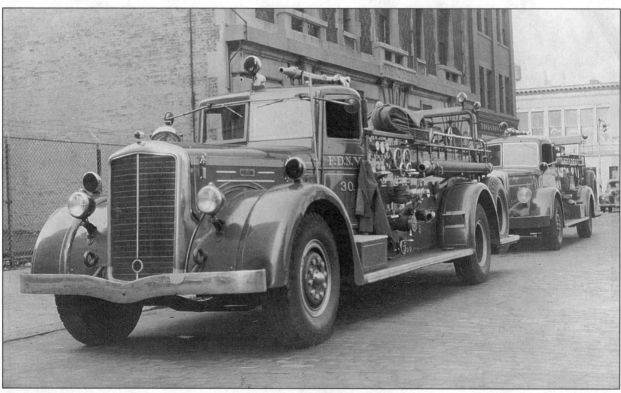

Engine 30 was this 1,000-gpm Ward LaFrance pumper It has a mounted deck gun and enclosed cab with "V" windshield. Behind it is a 1940 Mack Type 19 LS hose wagon.

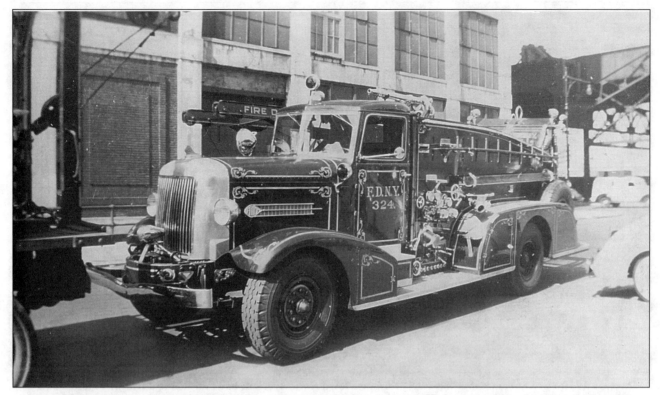

Several large cities, most notably Milwaukee, Wisconsin, built — or assembled — complete apparatus in their fire department shops. Here is FDNY's attempt, which appeared in 1939. The body was designed by the shops and fabricated by Ward LaFrance. The rig was powered by a Hercules engine and carried a 1,000-gpm American LaFrance pump. Costs turned out to be three times that of a purchased pumper and this was the only one built. It was assigned to Engine 324.

In view from rear note subway straps and rear suction inlet.

Wayne Sorensen Collection

This is a 1939 Ward LaFrance that was FDNY's first enclosed rescue truck. It had four doors, a two-way radio, and a 5-ton crane above the rear step. It ran as Rescue 1 and was stationed with Engine 30. In 1947 it was in an accident and required extensive rebuilding.

This 1940 Mack was originally a hose wagon and was then converted to a power supply van.

Frank J. Fenning photo

Engine 53's hose wagon was this 1940 Mack Type 19-LS. It has a mounted deck gun.

J. J. Lerch photo

This is a 1940 Ahrens-Fox with a spring-hoist 85-foot aerial ladder that was one of four purchased at the same time. It was Ladder 40. The tractor was rebuilt after being damaged in a building collapse.

Chapter 6

1941-1950

This was the decade of World War II. In 1940 and 1941 London had been subjected to punishing air raids and once the United States entered the war there was general concern that New York City would be one of the first targets for Nazi bombs. The Germans bombed indiscriminately in the sense that "bombs fell everywhere," meaning that a conventional fire department would be spread too thinly to fight fires at the site of each and every bomb blast.

Auxiliary Civil Defense units were formed that trained usually once a week. Some used their firefighting training at their places of employment —

they were expected to combat the flames until the city's equipment arrived. Other groups were trained to augment regular firefighters. Small pumping units, mounted on trailers and carrying a small pump, a length of suction hose, a reel of discharge hose, plus extinguishers, axes, and shovels, were stationed throughout the city and they could be attached to any auto.

Individual building owners were also expected to do their part. "Blackout" drills were conducted to make certain that no light was leaking out that might help enemy bombers find their targets. Sometimes, "blackout" curtains were installed. In

This mid-1940s Mack served as Engine 152. It's at a fire, keeping two hose lines supplied. This was a war model, as illustrated by its lack of chrome.

the top floor of buildings, shovels and buckets of sand were kept to fight fires that might be started by incendiary bombs (water wouldn't work on incendiaries, they burned too hot).

FDNY converted five old aerial ladder trucks to hose carriers that carried 3,000 feet of 4 1/2-inch hose each. Painted gray to make them less visible from the air, they were to be used when bombs destroyed water mains. A standup van was equipped as a traveling laboratory to test the air for possible poisonous gases and fumes. Fortunately, New York was not bombed and we never got to test the effectiveness of these defensive measures.

In 1943, small radios similar to military "walkie talkie" radios were issued to Rescue One.

Design of new apparatus for this decade can be placed into two categories: prewar and postwar. Prewar apparatus were, obviously, delivered before the war. A few new pieces trickled through during the war (especially if they could be justified for protecting a defense plant). One notable wartime delivery to FDNY was a Mack truck with a Heil 1,250-gallon tank body used for refueling. FDNY stationed two tank trucks in Manhattan and one in Brooklyn. They responded to all third alarms. At the war's end, prewar designs of apparatus were built and delivered. The first major "new" post-war design was the American LaFrance 700 series, introduced in 1947. Its front seat was placed forward of the engine and, eventually, nearly all makers of custom apparatus would follow.

In mid-1945, an Army Air Corps B25, flying from Boston to Newark, New Jersey, and lost in the fog, crashed into the 78th and 79th floors of the Empire State Building. Flames climbed nearly 10 stories higher. Luckily the accident occurred on a Saturday since that meant there were fewer workers within the building.

In December, 1946, in an abandoned ice house blaze, a wall collapsed onto an adjoining tenement, killing 38 people, including one fireman. During the decade there were several spectacular fires involving ships moored at New York piers. In 1942, the vessel Normandie burned at Pier 48. At a 1948 fire at Pier 57 over 150 firemen were overcome by smoke inhalation due to burning creosote.

In 1948, a selective transmitter was installed that sounded alarms only at the stations needed to fight the fire. Johnson wrote: "This reduced operating costs and at the same time eliminated one cause of hypertension and heart ailments among firemen. . ."[1]

In 1949, FDNY purchased 10 of these International KB series tractors to hitch to older aerial ladders, such as the 75-foot American LaFrance shown here.

1. Johnson, page 164

This is a 1941 Ward LaFrance Turret Wagon that ran as part of Engine 31. It was one of six.

This 1941 Ward LaFrance hose wagon was converted by the FDNY shops to a Rescue Squad. It ran as Squad 5. Note the floodlights on cab's roof.

A 1942 Walter with a heavy-duty wrecker/recovery body.

A 1943 International K used as Emergency No. 3 rescue truck. This picture was probably taken when the truck was old because "Michigan measles" are spreading along the bottom of the body.

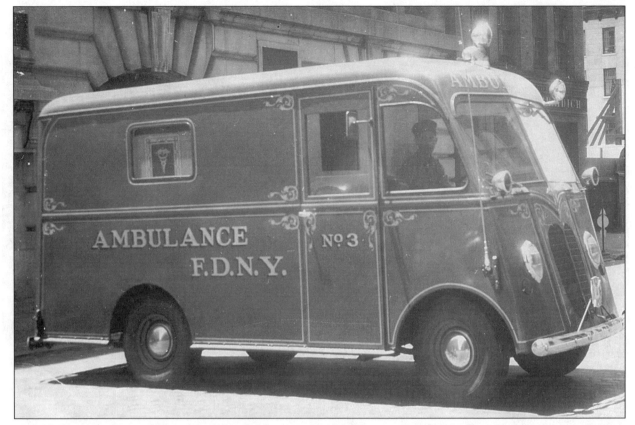

Ambulance No. 3 was this step van, probably an early 1940s International. Initially it had served as a field chemical laboratory unit.

This is a wartime 1944 Mack 1,000-gpm pumper with virtually no chrome. It ran as Engine 28.

This is one of 20 Ward LaFrance 750-gpm pumpers, an early post-war delivery. This one had a 200-gallon booster tank and a 100-gpm booster pump. Note the front suction intake on the far side, below the headlight. This one served as Engine 159.

This 1946 Ward LaFrance 750-gpm pumper was converted to a foam unit. It's shown in 1968, stationed at Engine 292.

Charles Beckwith Collection

This is one of 20 1947 American-LaFrance 700 series 750-gpm pumpers purchased by the FDNY. Note the deck gun and subway straps. These engines did not carry a booster tank. Note the cab-forward design that eventually would be offered by virtually all apparatus builders. (American-LaFrance had actually offered a cab-forward design as early as 1939.) One of its main advantages was improved driver visibility.

One of these 20 was assigned as Engine 9. It's shown here from the driver's side.

This view is from the curb side and shows the pump controls.

This 1946-48 DeSoto served as a chief's car. Number "7" is inside medallion.

Jack Robrecht photo

Flxible is a well-known bus builder and just after World War II it introduced its "airporter" model. This chassis and body appear similar except that it was equipped for ambulance use by the FDNY. It could transport six patients on stretchers. It also carried 28 cots that could be used at an aid station, and had its own generator, sterilizer, oxygen supply, hot water tank and heating pads. It also could hook up to outside power sources.

This 1948 Ward LaFrance tractor was one of 20 purchased to repower older aerials and water towers. This one is shown pulling a FEMCO 65-foot water tower.

Engine 38 was a 1947 Mack L series Model 85 with a 750-gpm pump and mounted deck gun.

This 1947 Ward LaFrance tractor was one of 20 purchased to power older aerial ladder trucks. This one is coupled to a 1941 Seagrave 75-foot aerial and was FDNY Truck 151.

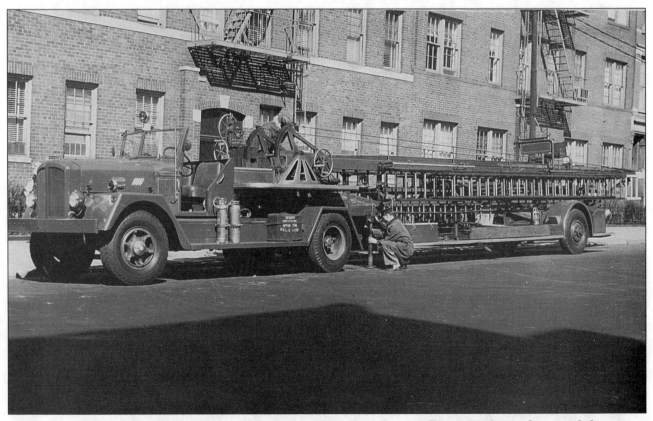

Here's another of the 20 Ward LaFrance 1947 tractors. This one is shown pulling a wooden 85-foot aerial that was originally coupled with a 1936 FWD tractor.

This 1948 Pirsch 85-foot metal aerial was one of three purchased. This one was assigned to run as Ladder 4.

Ladder 24 was the 85-foot, all-metal American LaFrance 700 series. The ladder was operated hydraulically, requiring only one firefighter, rather that an entire crew, to raise it. The tillerman's seat is in a fixed position to the rear of the lowered ladder.

J. J. Lerch photo

Ladder 110 was a 1948 Seagrave model J-85. It was FDNY's first metal aerial and was 85 feet long

The view from the rear shows the tillerman's seat, which has a windshield and windshield wiper.

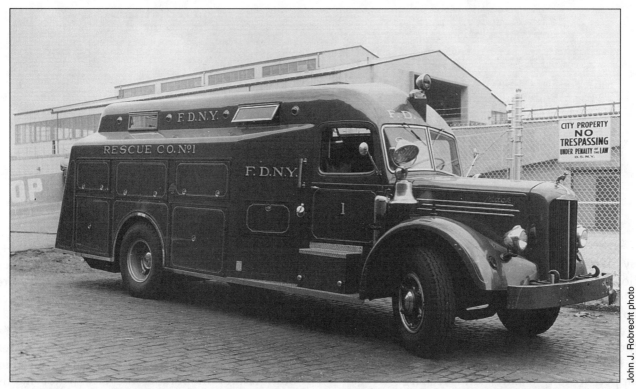

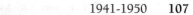

John J. Robrecht photo

FDNY's Rescue Company 1 used this 1948 Mack with an enclosed body built by the Approved Fire Equipment Co.

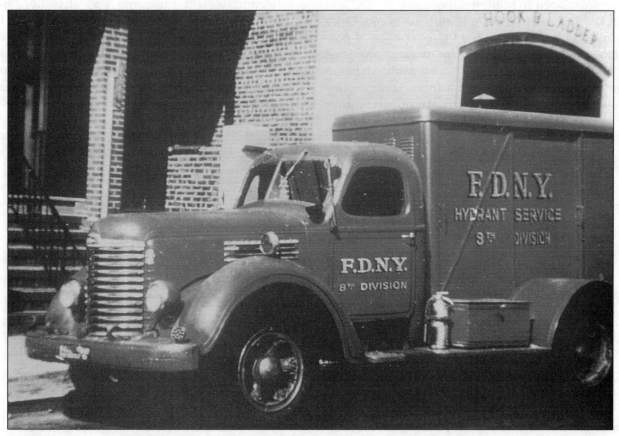

This 1949 International KB series served as the hydrant service truck in FDNY's 8th Division. Currently, there are more than 70,000 hydrants that FDNY can draw upon.

Chapter 7

1951-1960

By 1952 all FDNY apparatus had two-way radios. This, and the widespread use of telephones inside residences, lessened the need for the traditional fire-alarm box at every corner.

Breathing apparatus also made it easier for firefighters to enter and stay inside burning buildings and fight fires from the inside. In 1957, FDNY equipped a van to carry and recharge oxygen masks in the field.

The Cold War had begun and some of the World War II Civil Defense measures were brought back. There was one major difference: During World War II, the fear was that there would be many small bombs, dropped in scattered locations. In the Cold War, the fear was of a single nuclear bomb. Once again, New York was on the top of any list of possible enemy targets. Federal funds were provided so that large metropolitan areas could develop plans for coping with nuclear attacks. Some money was also allowed for the purchase of new equip-

ment. For several decades dwellers in large cities had to fear nuclear attacks. While those days are over, different types of attacks are now matters of legitimate concern and worry.

Gus Johnson wrote that on August 12, 1951; "a test was conducted to determine whether water could be brought to the city in case an air raid should render inoperable the city water mains that supply hydrants. It was necessary to devise a practical system. This was done by using quick-connecting eight-inch steel pipe of the type used during World War II to carry gasoline from the beachheads to the invading Allied armies. One thousand feet of this pipe was stretched along West Street. One end was connected to the fireboat, and from the other end, nine effective firefighting streams were delivered through 1 1/2-inch controlling nozzles. The results demonstrated that the Department could supply adequate water to any part of the City, regardless of

Wayne Sorensen Collection

Engine Company 96 ran this 1951 Ward LaFrance quad, equipped with a 750-gpm pump and a 250-gallon booster tank. It was one of a purchase of seven. Note the partial covering of the radiator to speed engine warming in cold weather.

damage to water mains."[1] In 1955, FDNY offered training sessions in radiology, in part because of concern over possible nuclear attacks and the possibilities of radioactive fallout. Traffic signs indicating evacuation routes became common in large cities.

Searchlight No. 2 ran in this 1960 International.

The view of the rear shows the lights. The photo was taken in Syracuse in 1999 at the S.P.A.A.M.F.A.A (Society for the Preservation and Appreciation of Antique Motor Fire Apparatus in America) annual meeting.

1. Johnson, page 168.

Frank J. Fenning photo

The FDNY shops built this hose wagon on a 1951 International chassis to run with Engine 159. On running board it carries backpack pumps.

Wayne Sorensen Collection

This 1951 Ward LaFrance pumper was rated at 750 gpm and had a 250-gallon booster tank. This is Engine 314, one of an order of 20.

Engine 304 was this 1952 Ward LaFrance 750-gpm pumper with 250-gallon booster tank and it ran as part of a two-piece unit. It was part of an order of 42.

This is a 1952 International B that FDNY shops built as a hose wagon to be used by Engine 159. Some parts on it had been taken off of older apparatus that was being retired.

This is a 1952 Ward LaFrance 750-gpm pumper and 250-gallon booster tank assigned to run as Civil Defense Engine 65. "Civil Defense" is written on the hood and the "CD" emblem is ahead of the rear wheels. Federal funding helped cities buy additional equipment that, conceivably, could be of help in case of an enemy air attack. The plywood roof and canvas covering over the hose bed were added later, in the 1960s, for riot protection.

International "Metro" vans were built as stand-up delivery trucks. FDNY bought two of these 1953 models for use as communications units. The side windows at the rear were added.

Ladder 26 was one of three 85-foot aerials purchased from Pirsch in 1953.

This 1953 Ward LaFrance engine has a 750-gpm pump and a booster tank. It was one of 39 purchased. This one is Engine 75. Plywood and tarpaulin coverings were added later as protection against rioters.

This is one of 20 85-foot aerials that were supplied by American LaFrance in 1953. Note there are no side doors on cabs — unique for this style. There is a grab bar to the side of the windshield. The truck pictured was Ladder Co. 102.

This is Ladder 109 from the same batch of 20. The photos may have been taken several years apart. Ladder 102 has turn indicators below the windshield and red lights above the bumper.

Wayne Sorensen Collection

Two 1953 Internationals were outfitted by the George Diehl Body Co. to be rescue trucks. This one ran as Rescue Co. 4.

Here's a view from the curb side. All the equipment was carried in compartments or inside the truck.

In 1954, FDNY bought 25 Mack Type 19HP 1,000-gpm pumpers. They did not have booster pumps. This one ran as Engine 16.

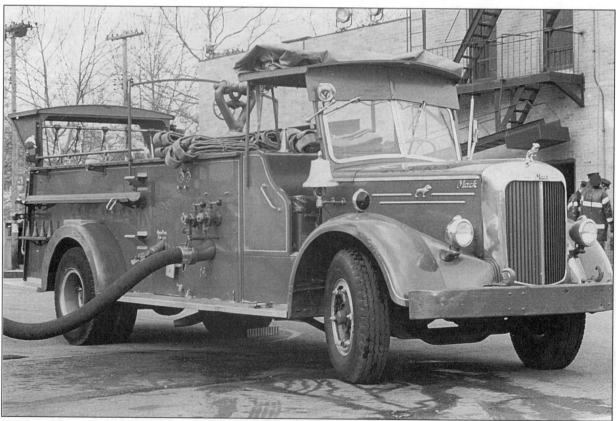

Here is a similar Mack from the same 1954 purchase, after it had been equipped with protection against rioters. At the rear is a plywood roof protecting firefighters riding in the rear. Plywood was also added over the windshield and front seat. Barely visible beyond the deck gun is a rod to support a tarpaulin that is to be stretched over the hose bed, protecting it from burning devices.

Here's a rear-angle view of Engine 27, another of the 25 Macks bought in 1954.

This 1954 Mack L Series pumper was converted into a satellite hose wagon for use in the Super-Pumper system (to be introduced in 1965). Protective covering has been provided for crew and hose bed. Eventually a number of apparatus would be designated as "Satellite." They carried hose, had deck guns, and accompanied large pumpers.

The George Diehl Body Co. built two of these searchlight trucks on 1954 International chassis. The one pictured is Searchlight No. 4.

This is a 1954 Ward LaFrance 750-gpm pumper, one of 25 purchased. It was carried on the Civil Defense roster as Engine 45.

Wayne Sorensen Collection

This is the fireboat "John D. McKean" built in 1954 at the John Mathis Shipyards, in Camden, New Jersey. It could pump 19,000 gpm and had seven monitors, including one in the tower that was controlled remotely.

This is Ladder 163, a 1956 FWD, after riot protection roofs have been added. Note especially the roof protecting the tillerman.

In 1956, FDNY acquired 11 of the American LaFrance 85-foot aerials. This one was Ladder 108. Photos of other American LaFrance apparatus of this era show that on this order of trucks the windshields are higher and at a less rakish angle.

This is Ladder 15, a 75-foot wooden aerial pulled by a 1956 FWD tractor. It was one of 25 purchased by FDNY. Built with Douglas fir, these were the last wooden aerials that FDNY would buy.

This was a mobile medical emergency unit carried in a bus body.

Four 1958 International "Metros" were equipped by the George Diehl Body Co. to run as Squads. This one was Squad Unit No. 1.

Engine 275 was one of 13 1,000-gpm Mack C95F pumpers acquired in 1959.

Here's a curbside view of Engine 65, another of the 13 1959 Mack pumpers.

This 1959 Mack C 85 chassis pulls a semi-trailer with a Maxim 85-foot aerial ladder. It's Ladder 10 and was one of 11 bought at the same time.

Here's a rear view of another of the 11 1959 Mack ladder trucks. This was also after installation of protective roofs over both the cab and tilllerman's seat.

This is Engine 40, one of 16 Ward LaFrance "Firebrand" models with 1,000-gpm pumps, purchased in 1960.

Rescue 1 was built on a 1959 Mack chassis by Gerstenslager. In the photo the equipment doors are shown open and they are casting a shadow on the truck's side.

This 1960 Ward LaFrance "Firebrand" ran as Squad No. 2.

This 1960 Ward LaFrance "Firebrand" was photographed toward the end of its service, it was designated as a spare to fill in for another piece of apparatus that was in the shops.

Chapter 8

1961-1970

This was a decade that started on a high note, with the inauguration of President John F. Kennedy. By the middle of the decade, the nation was involved in the war in Vietnam. At home there were peaceful protests that turned into ugly riots. In large cities, firefighters responding to alarms were pelted with rocks, bottles, and flaming devices. Some were even shot at.

Fire departments, including FDNY, added plywood roofs above the seats and rear platform to protect the firefighters. Tent-like canvasses were used to protect the hose bed from flaming missiles.

Apparatus historians will be looking at this equipment a century from now will probably wonder why suddenly it became necessary to add these temporary roofs. By the end of 1968 in New York City, 240 pumpers and 120 ladder trucks had been equipped with protective coverings. Some other open apparatus was retired early.

In 1962, the three refueling trucks were converted into water tankers with booster pumps for use in outlying areas where wild land fires occurred. Contracts were entered into with private companies to provide the refueling services. (How

This is Ladder 120 that in 1965 was FDNY's busiest ladder company, making more than 6,000 runs in that year. The truck is a Seagrave with a 100-foot aerial. Note that it has no doors. The truck was one of an order of eight.

Wayne Sorensen Collection

long this policy lasted is unknown. Note that we show pictures of an FDNY refueler purchased in 1989.) Diesel engines had been introduced for trucks just before World War II. After World War II, they became much more common on fire apparatus and eventually took the place of gasoline-powered apparatus engines.

By 1965, there were more than 13,200 men in the department. One reason for the increase in personnel over the years was that the firefighters' hours of work per week were being reduced. By 1969 the roster would increase to over 14,000.

The major apparatus news in this decade was the design and acquisition of the "super-pumper." This pumper, carried on a trailer, was likened to a land-based fireboat with tremendous pumping capacity. It could move huge quantities of water at pressure so great that walls would collapse or stacked lumber would be scattered. There were also three satellite tenders that worked with the super-pumper. John Calderone wrote that the super-pumper "concept was a sound one, but limited in application."[1]

Another innovative piece of apparatus acquired by FDNY in the 1960s was the aerial platform on a telescopic boom. The boom was more flexible than a conventional aerial ladder, could move vertically and horizontally, could lift equipment and firefighters and move people on stretchers.

In 1966, 12 FDNY firefighters lost their lives when a floor collapsed during a five-alarm fire at Broadway at 22nd and 23rd Streets. At the time it was the largest loss of FDNY lives in a single incident.

The year 1968 was a bad year for riots and other disturbances in major cities, and New York City was no exception. Protesters often set trash on fire and this resulted in many alarms tying up both firemen and equipment. Old and abandoned buildings were torched. False alarms were common. Some fire companies were overworked to the extent that they were "paired" with less active companies in outlying stations and would then exchange station assignments. Firemen and engines were pelted with stones, rubbish and Molotov cocktails. In some areas, apparatus would respond in convoys for "self-protection." Temporary protective covers were added to most apparatus to shelter both firemen and hose beds. Equipment purchased subsequently would provide completely protected seats for firefighters. Equipment was stowed inside locked cabinets to prevent rioters from stealing it.

Since 9/11, one cannot help but contrast the differences in admiration and respect that is felt for FDNY firefighters now and in the late 1960s.

Engine Co. 60 was one of 74 engine companies to receive a new Mack CF pumper in 1970. The engine had a 1,000-gpm pump and a 400-gallon booster tank.

1. John A. Calderone, *The History of Fire Engines* (Greenwich, CT: Brompton, 1997), p. 64.

A 1961 Chevrolet Viking used as a salvage truck by Fire Patrol 3. The canvas roof may have been added after riots.

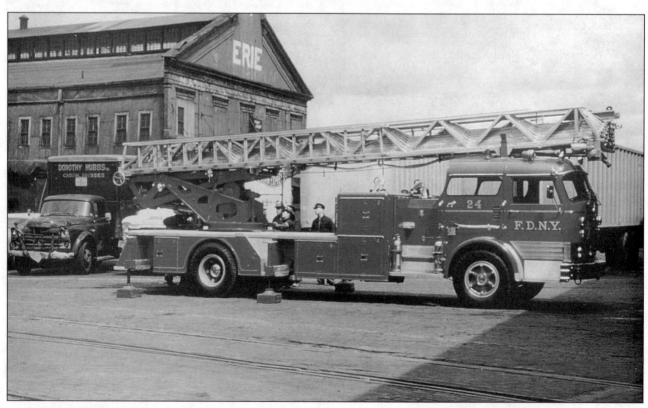

Outriggers are extended on Ladder 24, a 1961 Mack with its seven-section, 146-foot Magirus ladder

This 1954 Mack foam truck was originally a pumper.

Searchlight No. 1 was a 1959 Mack with a body outfitted by H & H Body Company of Jersey City. It has eight portable lights.

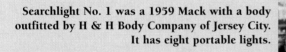

Engine 44 was a 1958 Mack equipped with automatic transmissions and had 750-gpm Hale pumps.

Searchlight No. 2 was a 1960 International.

Don Wood photo

Engine 209 was a 1969 1,000-gpm pumper with a crew cab and "covered wagon" tarpaulin to protect the hose bed.

Ladder 84 was a 1970 diesel-powered Seagrave rear-mount aerial.

Wayne Sorensen Collection

Ladder 18 was a 100-foot Seagrave rear-mount aerial that FDNY bought in 1971.

Ladder Co. 127 was a 1972 Mack with a Baker 75-foot tower ladder.

Harlem's Engine 69, a 1980 American LaFrance, works on a Manhattan fire in 1991.

Warren Weiss photo

This 1980 American LaFrance hose tender was originally a pumper.

Engine 46 was a 1981 Mack CF with a 1,000-gpm pump and 500-gallon tank. It was part of FDNY's brief experiment with the lime-green color.

Warren Weiss photo

Rescue 3 used a 1983 American LaFrance/Saulsbury for "collapse rescue."

Joseph A. Pinto photo

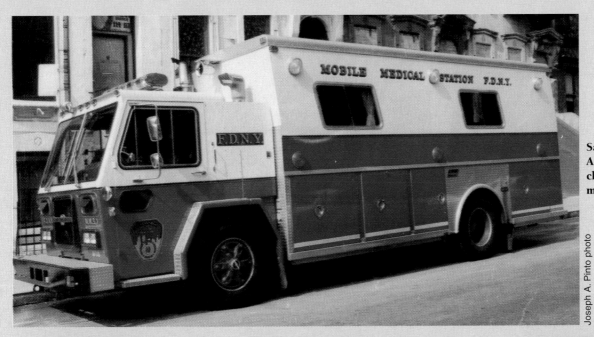

Saulsbury used a 1983 American LaFrance chassis for its mobile medical station.

Ladder 34 used a 1988 Seagrave that carried a tillered 100-foot aerial ladder.

This hazardous-materials response truck rode on a 1990 Amertek chassis with off-road capability.

134

Ladder Co. 44 ran this 1991 Mack with a 95-foot boom.

Joseph A. Pinto photo

Tower Ladder 54, stationed in the Bronx, used a 1995 FWD with a Saulsbury body and Baker 75-foot aerialscope.

Warren Weiss photo

Satellite 5 responds to a four-alarm fire on Staten Island in 1999. In the background is Tower Ladder 77.

Warren Weiss photo

Nearly 100 FDNY vehicles were lost in the World Trade Center disaster. Here, a badly damaged aerial ladder is on the left and an overturned emergency vehicle is on its side.

911 Pictures

Following the 9/11 disaster, a burned-out hulk of a piece of apparatus is on the right, while an active tower is behind.

911 Pictures

911 Pictures

When the World Trade Center collapsed, dust was everywhere, and it was mixed with smoke coming from smoldering ruins. Diesel engines on some apparatus "choked" because of all the dust their cooling systems sucked in.

The 9/11 disaster will be remembered mainly for its toll in lives and loss of real estate. FDNY also took a major "hit" in terms of lost apparatus. A battalion chief's vehicle is in the foreground while a tower ladder in the background surveys one portion of the disaster site.

911 Pictures

This is a 2002 Seagrave rear-mount aerial built for FDNY. Employees of Seagrave paid for the American flag design.

Brett Romberg, Seagrave photo

This was "High Ladder No. 1," a 1961 Mack C85 chassis carrying a rear-mount seven-section 146-foot Magirus ladder. It was one of two.

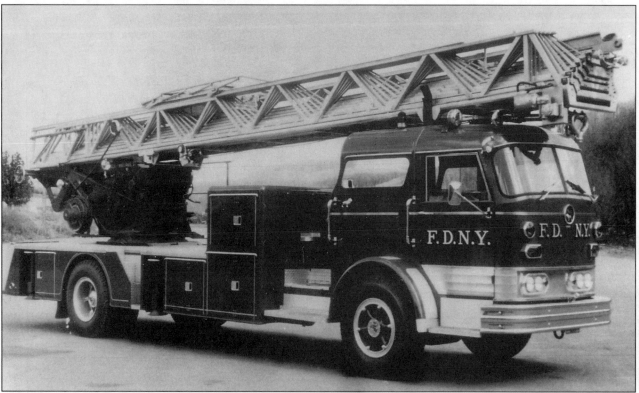

This is a factory photo showing similar apparatus from the curb side.

Here's a front view of the apparatus after the 146-foot Magirus ladder was replaced in 1969 with a 100-foot Grove ladder.

This is Ladder 115, a 1961 Mack with a 100-foot Grove aerial ladder that had replaced a 146-foot Magirus ladder.

Ladder 26 was a 100-foot American LaFrance aerial, one of seven received in 1962.

Engine 10 was this Mack C95F with a 1,000-gpm pump and 375-gallon booster tank and covered cab. It was part of an order of 11. A single spotlight extends above the center of the windshield.

H & H Body Company outfitted this 1963 International chassis with a 1,000-gpm pump and body to serve as Engine 290.

FDNY used this 1963 heavy-duty L Series International wrecker/recovery vehicle with what is probably a Holmes twin-boom body.

Engine 35 was a 1963 International with an H & H body. It was one of 10 purchased.

This 1963 International with an H & H body and 1,000-gpm capacity has "fought the good fight" as both Engine 73 and Engine 298. Here we see it after it has been condemned to scrapping and stripped of all moveable equipment.

A 1964 Mack C 85 chassis was used to carry a 75-foot "aerialscope," a telescopic boom, built by Traco. The boom could be used to move firefighters and equipment, or lower victims. The truck was designated "Tower Ladder No. 1."

The best-known single piece of apparatus built during the 1960s was FDNY's "Super-Pumper." William Francis Gibbs, a navel architect, designed the unit to function almost as a fireboat, capable of pumping huge streams of water at major conflagrations. It was designed to take the place of 10 conventional pumpers at the site of a fire. A 1965 Mack tractor pulled a trailer carrying a six-stage DeLaval pump that could pump 8,800 gpm at 350 psi.

Here's Tower Ladder No. 1 at a stubborn warehouse fire. Two aerial ladders can be seen at the right.

Here is a rear view of the Super-Pumper at work. In the center rear of the trailer is a winch and crane used for handling the heavy hoses that are connected to the pumper.

Mack also built a large hose tender to work with the Super-Pumper. The tractor carrier a Stang 8-inch monitor and a 2,000-gpm fog tip that could be fed by four 4 1/2-inch hoses. The tractor could be operated independently of the hose trailer and the tractor had hydraulic stabilizing outriggers to steady it when the monitor was in use. The trailer carried 2,000 feet of 4 1/2-inch hose.

This is one of three 1965 Mack C series, diesel-powered satellite hose tenders. It carried a Stang "Intelligiant" monitor with a 6-inch barrel that was manually controlled and 2,000 feet of 4 1/2-inch hose.

This is a Satellite 3 at work on a cold winter day. Ice is everywhere, but firemen have scraped it off of the cab door so that it doesn't freeze shut.

Satellite tender 3 is at the right, at a church fire.

The Super-Pumper and its satellites at work.

This 1965 American LaFrance 100-foot aerial was one of 12 purchased. They were powered by Cummins diesel engines. This one ran as Ladder No. 26.

This is Engine 13, a 1965 diesel-powered Mack with a 1,000-gpm pump, a booster system, and a deck gun.

This 1965 Mack C series was extensively rebuilt by Comcoach in 1977 and became a satellite. The components that survived the rebuild were the chassis, power train, Stang monitor, and piping. The new body and equipment compartments were made of fiberglass, and the rebuilt truck bore little resemblance to the original. This rig ran as Satellite 4.

This is the FDNY tender "Smoke," a small boat used by the Marine battalion chief, and to change crews of fire boats operating at a fire.

Wayne Sorensen Collection

In 1968, FDNY accepted 12 of these American LaFrance 100-foot aerials. They were diesel-powered and had automatic transmissions. This one served as Ladder 158.

This is Truck 115 carrying a Magirus 100-foot aerial.

FDNY ordered 20 of these 1968 Mack series CF pumpers. Note the herculite covering over the hose bed, protecting it from Molotov cocktails and other flaming missiles. The backward-facing seats at the rear of the cab were enclosed and protected by doors. Note the front suction.

This is a 1969 American LaFrance with a 100-foot rear-mount aerial ladder. It ran as Tactical Control Unit 732.

In this view from the rear we see two of the stabilizing outrigger jacks.

Ten 1969 Mack MB tractors were purchased to replace tractors on older aerials. This one, Ladder 115, was coupled with a 100-foot Grove aerial. Sheet-metal reinforcements have been placed in lower front corners of cab probably to prevent — or cover — dents.

This 1969 Mack tractor pulls a 1948 Pirsch 85-foot aerial. It's Ladder 85 and was stationed with Engine 165. Note the front of the station.

Wayne Sorensen Collection

Ed Gardner photo

This 1969 Mack tractor was converted to a high-expansion foam unit in 1977.

This 1969 Mack also was originally purchased to tow an older aerial ladder; instead it became a twin-boom wrecker/recovery vehicle.

Engine 218 was part of an order of 35 1969 Mack series CF pumpers. They were diesel-powered and rated at 1,000-gpm.

This is a side view of another of the fleet of 35. In center background we see a fire training tower.

This view from the rear shows shelter provided for firemen riding at the rear. Looking beyond the pump is a fireman riding on the rear-mounted seat also protected by a door.

Engine 209 was one of five 1969 Mack R-model 1,000-gpm pumpers. It has a crew cab and "covered wagon" tarpaulin to protect the hose bed.

The pump panel on 1968-69 Macks used by FDNY.

In 1969, FDNY purchased four Mack 75-foot towers with Eaton booms. This one was Ladder 119.

This is Ladder 172, with its boom lowered almost to the ground.

This 1969 Seagrave rear-mount 100-foot aerial was a demonstrator. It carried some extra chrome.

FDNY purchased this Seagrave to serve as Ladder 27, second section.

Ladder 84 was one of 21 diesel-powered Seagrave rear-mount aerials that FDNY purchased in 1970.

Because of manning requirements it was necessary to add an additional enclosed riding space at a midship position along the curb side. It was nicknamed the "telephone booth" for obvious reasons.

Chapter 9

1970-1980

Absentee landlords, drugs, and social unrest continued at the start of the 1970s. In the early 1970s some companies made 7,000 to 8,000 runs per year. It was not uncommon for men in some firehouses to catnap on their rigs through the night, as they got tired out from going up and down to their bunk rooms.[1] In 1976, there were 13,752 arson fires, an all-time high (by way of comparison, in 1984 the figure was 5,157). Some arson fires were (and are) related to hate and were aimed at people of color or synagogues.

Some apparatus with enclosed cabs had door locks because, apparently, in some situations a stranger could climb into an engine at a fire site and drive it away. Rescue One was assigned a Hurst Tool, known as the "Jaws of Life," used to cut away parts of autos or transit vehicles in order to rescue their occupants.

In the 1970s, New York City faced a major financial crisis. In 1973, there was a 5 1/2-hour strike by FDNY's firemen. There were cutbacks in all city operations, including FDNY. A number of compa-

This is Ladder 18. It was one of an order of 13 100-foot Seagrave rear-mount aerials that FDNY bought in 1971.

nies were deactivated, some on a temporary, roving basis.

Changes in manning formulas reduced the number of firefighters assigned to each piece of equipment.

Johnson wrote: "In 1975 the super-pumper ceased to be a separate unit. The pumper was hereafter to be manned by the members of Engine company 207. . . . In an effort to reduce the unnecessary running by Battalion Chiefs, fire-alarm boxes with a long record of false alarms and alarms for fires not occurring in buildings were designated as discretionary response boxes (D.R.B.). On alarms from these boxes the Battalion Chief waits until a preliminary report is received, and responds only when the fire is in a building. Almost one thousand firemen were laid off in a fiscal crisis and the ruthless paring down of the Department that resulted."[2] Equipment purchases were also cut back. Local neighborhoods protested the closing of "their" stations.

In February, 1975, there was a major fire in the World Trade Center. It was on the 11th floor, although there was minor damage along the building's core stretching from floors 9 through 11. In mid-June there was an epidemic of 40 fires within three hours in the South Bronx. It was believed that they were set in protest of President Ford's veto of an emergency jobs bill. BBC ran a documentary entitled "The Bronx is Burning." In August, 1978,

six firefighters were killed and 31 injured at a supermarket fire in Brooklyn when the building's roof collapsed.

One major change in the fire apparatus field which occurred in the 1970s was the introduction of a lime green color (National Safety Yellow) to take the place of traditional red. The lime green was more easily seen under conditions of darkness. Nearly every department, when buying new apparatus, would have to decide if it wanted to choose the new color. FDNY had one pumper painted lime green (nicknamed "The Green Apple") and ordered some others, but did not adopt that color. There was fierce resistance from firefighters as well as much of the general public who wanted to keep the traditional red. They argued that during daylight hours, the bright red was more likely to be associated with fire apparatus than a truck painted some strange hue of wimpy greenish-yellow. Calderone wrote: "The lack of recognition of the new color was documented as a contributing factor in accidents involving lime green apparatus. It seemed that after initial delivery, keeping up the shiny, bright appearance of the color was not as easy as to keep up the red, and these vehicles didn't instill the pride that the traditionally painted trucks has in the fire service."[3]

A change in firefighters' gear was the introduction of the self-contained breathing apparatus. Flame-retardant clothing was also adopted.

This 1972 Mack, Ladder Co. 127, had a Baker 75-foot tower ladder. It was one of 20.

2. Johnson, p. 214.
3. Calderone, p. 90.

Rescue 4 was built by Providence Body Company on a 1971 diesel-powered Mack R chassis.

This 1971 Mack CF was a tower ladder and carried a 75-foot Baker Boom (aerialscope). There were doors protecting the occupants of the rearward-facing crew sets. This is Ladder 13, one of eight purchased.

In the 1970s, the National Park Service outfitted this all-wheel drive Ford with beefed-up suspension, flotation tires and a Pacific pump to fight off-road fires in the Gateway National Recreation Area in New York City. It was justified, in part, to avoid charges the FDNY assessed the federal government for fighting fires on federal lands. The rig was nicknamed "Mini-Super-Pumper," a takeoff on the name of the humongous New York City pumping unit.

National Park Service photo

A 1979 GMC General with a Weld Built wrecker/recovery body. It was one of the first FDNY trucks painted lime green and ran as Wrecker 3.

This 1978 Mack CF pumper was rated at 1,000 gpm and was one of an order of 40. Here we see it after it was converted to a foam unit. The roof over the rear protects firefighters.

This 1978 Mack, converted to a foam unit, has FDNY's newer colors.

Joseph A. Pinto photo

This is Ladder 34, one of five 1979 Seagrave 100-foot aerials. The cab is enclosed.

Engine 216 was one of 80 American LaFrance "Century" models with 1,000-gpm pumps.

Harlem's Engine 69 shown working at a two-alarm fire in Manhattan in 1991.

This 1980 American LaFrance pumper was converted to a hose tender.

This 1980 GMC with a Comcoach body was initially a salvage unit, and then converted to a hazardous materials team truck.

Chapter 10

1981-1990

Over the years fire apparatus used by FDNY (and everywhere else) has become much heavier, wider and higher. In many New York City locations, fire stations are hemmed in and cannot be expanded easily. (In the flood of TV shows featuring life at FDNY firehouses since 9/11, pictures of apparatus moving out of or backing into doors show the narrowest of clearances.)

In 1984, a report issued by FDNY indicated that apparatus painted lime green had a higher incidence of traffic accidents than apparatus painted red. Later that year, the green engine was repainted red. FDNY did, however, began adding a horizontal white stripe and white cabs to help make the apparatus more visible.

Hazardous materials incidents received increasing attention in the 1980s. Special equipment was developed, as was additional training for personnel. Firemen were concerned about being exposed to toxic hazards such as burning PCBs. After possible exposure at a fire, it was necessary to decontaminate both the firemen and their apparatus. FDNY established it as Hazardous Materials Rescue Unit No. 1, and based it in Queens.

Smoke detectors were required in apartments. There were many problems of arson and landlords allegedly burning out their existing tenants and then converting the buildings to expensive luxury apartments.

Warren Weiss photo

This 1981 Mack CF with a 1,000-gpm pump and 500-gallon tank was part of FDNY's brief experiment with the lime-green color. It was Engine 46. Later it would be painted red with some white.

Labor disputes also continued. In 1982, the Uniformed Firefighters Association filed suit in a Federal District Court claiming FDNY was not providing equal fire protection in all areas of the city. The union believed that a way to achieve more equal service would be to rescind some manpower cuts. The union began a series of "sick-outs" and "rule-book" slowdowns. Thousands of off-duty firemen marched down Broadway to City Hall where a rally was held to put pressure on Mayor Edward Koch. Many firemen also opposed efforts to open the department's ranks to females.

During much of the 1980s, there were "turf" wars between FDNY and New York's police department. At issue was which agency was in charge at a disaster or incident site? One example was underwater rescues from fallen helicopters. During the 1980s, Rescue One performed several rescues of people who had been strapped into helicopters that had fallen into the rivers. In 1988, the squad was equipped with a thermal imaging camera that could

detect different temperatures on the other side of a surface. In 1985, firefighters were given small signaling devices to carry. The devices would sound if the firefighter was motionless for 30 seconds and was intended to alert other firefighters that one of their brothers was down. (People performing rescue operations immediately following the WTC disaster heard some of these devices.)

On April 18, 1982, FDNY reportedly reduced the number of companies responding to automatic alarms at the World Trade Center.

There were numerous fires in subway cars, most of which started in the switchboxes under floors. On December 12, 1984, alone there were 16 subway fires; for all of 1984, the total topped 4,500. So many cars were involved that the number of trains operating was reduced. In mid-1985, Grand Central Terminal, a major commuter station, was closed for a morning rush hour because of fires started inside railcars. In March 1990 an arson fire at the Happyland Social Club in the Bronx took 87 lives.

This is a satellite hose wagon built by Saulsbury to be carried on a 1982 American LaFrance Century chassis. It carried large-diameter hose and cans of foam powder. Note the large monitor that could deliver 4,400 gpm. It ran as Satellite No. 1.

Joseph A. Pinto photo

This 1982 American LaFrance chassis carried an enclosed Saulsbury rescue/hazardous materials body with side and rear doors plus an escape hatch in the roof. It carried a large generator and quartz floodlights, plus drums for holding recovered hazardous wastes. It could also serve as a mobile command center. Most FDNY apparatus from this point forward have white tops to make them more visible at night.

Rescue 3 rode in this 1983 American LaFrance/Saulsbury. This was a "collapse rescue" equipped to be used at sites of building or tunnel collapses.

Adam Alberti photo

This 1983 American LaFrance pumper now serves as FDNY's caisson unit in funeral corteges. It will carry the casket of any FDNY member killed in the line of duty. In this 1998 picture we see on the left Scottish fifes and drummers and on the right uniformed firefighters are saluting their one-time comrade. Note that the truck has the newer style white top and "FIRE" lettering.

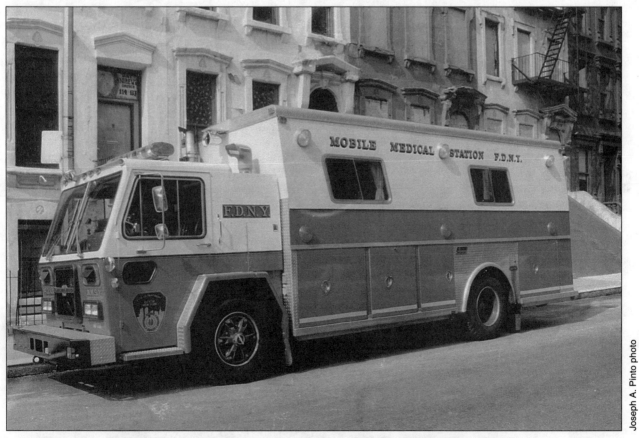

Joseph A. Pinto photo

Saulsbury built this mobile medical station on a 1983 American LaFrance chassis. It was one of two.

This 1984 GMC pickup is a brush rig and has a shop-built pump tank and hose-reel unit.

Rear view shows engine and rear of hose reels. Signs indicate the engine should not be run unless it is pumping water.

Adam Alberti photo

This Mack heavy-duty tow truck, from the mid-1980s, served as FDNY's Wrecker 3. Here it is parked outside the FDNY shops. It appears to have been around the block a few times.

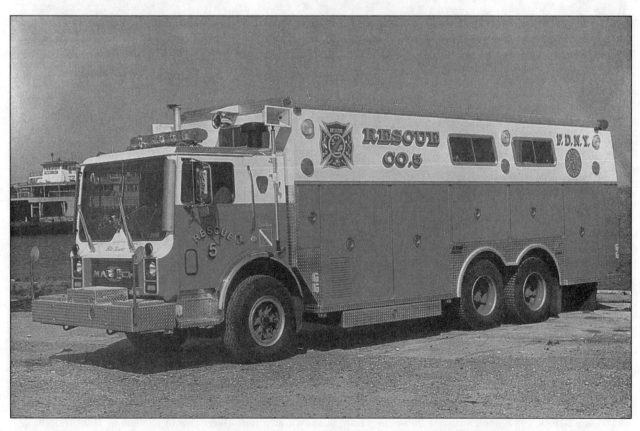

This is one of two 1985 Mack MCs with bodywork by Saulsbury used as Rescue Company 5. It has a 15-kilowatt generator and a rear-mounted winch and portable A-frame.

Joseph A. Pinto photo

This is a field communications unit in a Saulsbury-built body carried on 1985 Mack R chassis. The circular device above the closest corner is a mirror allowing the driver to see immediately in front of the truck. The twin towers of the World Trade Center are in background.

Warren Weiss photo

Engine 316, a 1985 Mack with a 1,000-gpm pump, is shown at a four-alarm fire in Queens in 1998. FDNY purchased 25 of this model in 1998.

Adam Alberti photo

This 1986 GMC brush rig is used on Staten Island. It carries a "slip-on" body on its all-wheel-drive flatbed chassis. Note the heavy bumper, grille guard and brush guard.

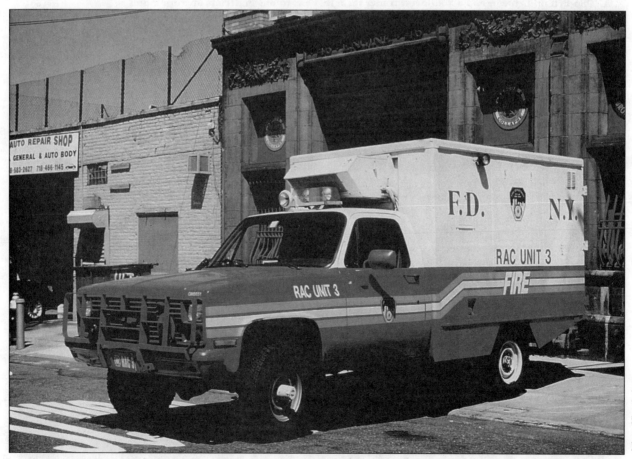

Adam Alberti photo

This is a RAC (recuperation and care) unit, used to treat exhausted firemen at the scene of fires. The FDNY shop-built body is mounted on a 1986 GMC chassis. Note that a golden orange horizontal stripe has been added, along with a different lettering style for the word "FIRE."

Joseph A. Pinto photo

A 1986 Peterbilt tractor and a Southwest trailer form this hazardous materials operation unit.

Warren Weiss photo

Note the Christmas boughs on the front of Engine 154, a 1986 Seagrave with a 100-foot, rear-mount aerial ladder. It has tandem rear wheels. It was one of the first deliveries with the upper portion of the cab painted white.

This is one of 18 1987 Mack CF series pumpers that FDNY bought. Ward79 built the bodies. The engines could pump 1,000 gpm. This was engine 93.

This is Engine 84, a 1987 Mack/Ward79. On the extended front bumper is some barely visible pre-connected 1 3/4-inch hose called the "trash" line. There is also front suction.

This 1987 Mack/Ward79 has been converted to foam unit No. 96. It has a 1,000-gallon tank.

Tower Ladder 33 is stationed in the Bronx. It's a 1987 Mack with a Baker 75-foot Aerialscope.

Tower Ladder 86 on Staten Island was a 1988 Mack with a 75-foot Baker Aerialscope. Note the stabilizing jacks in the front corners and between the front and rear wheels.

This 1988 Mack DM chassis carried a Weld Built tow body. It served as Wrecker No. 2.

Adam Alberti photo

Ladder 34 was this 1988 Seagrave that carried a tillered 100-foot aerial ladder. The sign on the door says "Where Harlem Reaches the Heights."

Joseph A. Pinto photo

This 1989 Ford had a Reading utility body modified by Saulsbury and was assigned to run as "Tactical Support No. 1." It carried a generator, elevating floodlights, an air compressor, hydraulic tools, and a rescue boat. Again note new style of "FIRE" lettering.

Joseph A. Pinto photo

A 1989 GMC flatbed outfitted by Saulsbury with a hydrant-thawing unit.

Adam Alberti photo

This is Engine 293, stationed in Queens, working at a fire. It's a 1989 Mack with a Ward79 body and has a 1,000-gpm pump and 500-gallon tank.

Engine 159 on Staten Island used this 1989 Mack CF outfitted with a Ward79 body. It could pump 2,000 gpm and carried 500 gallons of water.

This 1989 Mack tank truck carried diesel oil for refueling apparatus. It held 3,000 gallons. This one is white and red with a green tank.

A hazardous-materials response truck carried on a 1990 Amertek chassis with off-road capability.

Rescue 2 used this 1990 Mack/Saulsbury truck. The twin towers of the World Trade Center are in the background.

Chapter 11

1991-2000

In February of 1993 there was a major bomb explosion, set by terrorists, in the lower levels of the World Trade center. Six people were killed and more than 1,000 were injured. Approximately 50,000 people were evacuated from the WTC complex, including nearly 25,000 from each of the two towers. Fire alarm dispatchers received more that 1,000 phone calls, most reporting victims trapped on the upper floors of the towers. Search and evacuation of the towers finally were completed some 11 hours after the incident began.[1]

A nitrourea bomb weighing more than 1,000 lbs. and hydrogen cylinders were loaded into a rental Ryder Econoline van that was exploded on the B-2 level of the parking garage. The destruction spanned seven levels, most of them below ground. The crater was L-shaped and maximum measurements were 150 by 130 feet. FDNY sent 84 engine companies, 60 truck companies, 28 battalion chiefs, nine deputy chiefs, and five rescue companies and 26 other special units (representing nearly 45 percent of the on-duty staff of FDNY). The fire depart-

Joseph A. Pinto photo

Hazardous Materials Company 1 rode in a 1991 International with a body by Saulsbury. Equipment included chemical protective suits for use by the clean-up crew.

1. Anthony L. Fusco, "Report from Chief of Department," in *The World Trade Center Bombing Report and Analysis* (Washington. D.C.: Federal Emergency Management Agency, 1994) p. 1

ment units maintained a presence on the scene for 28 days.[2]

Two comments made by Chief Fusco indicate the difficulties encountered: "Operations continued well into the night. At 11:45 p.m., the last elevator was located and the people removed. They had been in the elevator for more than 11 hours." And "Change of tour relief would be handled by the transmission of additional alarms. Some members, due to the fact that they had climbed to the upper floors of the towers, could not be relieved. It took hours to reach the upper floors of the two 110-story buildings, and, of necessity, these members would be kept working until they could make their way down the buildings, performing secondary searches as necessary."[3]

Using perfect hindsight, one can see that the WTC served as a symbol of both the nation and the high-powered economic system that the terrorists wished to attack.

In 1996, New York City's Emergency Medical Service (EMS) was merged into the FDNY. This added over 4,000 people (including about 3,000 emergency medical technicians) to the FDNY roster.

Third Watch, a TV drama series on NBC, focused on intertwined action and personal lives of New York City fire, police, and EMS personnel. It focused with both their on-the-job experiences as well as their relationships with families, friends, and others.

The New York City Fire Museum, located in a renovated fire house at 278 Spring Street, had a display of FDNY firefighters' gear over the past several decades. For the 1990s, the museum noted: "Gone are the high boots and long turnout coat of earlier years, replaced by bunker gear that more completely protects the body; it consists of a matching jacket and pants of tear, fire, and water-resistant fabrics; blue suspenders, not red, hold up his pants. On his head, the same type of helmet as worn in the 1980s; strapped to his back is a newer version of the Scott Air-Pak which is much lighter than the 1970s version, with the weight carried on the hips, rather than the shoulders."[4]

In the year 2000, 99 firefighters died in the line of duty in the United States. Over the past decade, the number of deaths annually nationwide ranged between 75 and 112. This may help place in perspective the enormity of the tragedy on 9/11/01.

Tower Ladder 58, stationed in the Bronx, used this 1991 Mack CF with a Baker Aerialscope 95-foot boom and a Saulsbury body. In the windshield is a sign that says: "Bronx Champs."

Adam Alberti photo

2. Ibid., p. 2.
3. Ibid., p. 16
4. http://www.nycfiremuseum.org/newsletter/curators.htm (December 5, 2001).

This is a 1991 Mack chassis with the body off of a 1982 American LaFrance/Saulsbury rescue truck body that Saulsbury's factory placed onto the Mack chassis. It was in reserve and then pressed into service as Rescue 2 after the WTC disaster destroyed the equipment of Rescue 2 (and 3 and 4 and 5).

Ladder Co. 44 ran this 1991 Mack with a 95-foot boom.

Joseph A. Pinto photo

This is Ladder Company 40's 100-foot tillered ladder built by Seagrave. It was one of eight.

Joseph A. Pinto photo

This 1992 Mack, with twin rear axles and Saulsbury bodywork, was a 3,000-gallon foam tender.

Joseph A. Pinto photo

Engine 163 was one of a dozen 1992 Seagrave pumpers purchased by FDNY. It had a 1,000-gpm pump and carried 750 gallons of water.

This is a 1993 Mack MR with a Saulsbury body that has a monitor with 4,000-gpm capacity. It was one of six purchased. This one served as Satellite 2

Here is a similar model, Satellite 3, working at a fire. Note that it also carries cans of foam.

And this is Satellite 5, stationed on Staten Island.

Warren Weiss photo

Here is Satellite 5 working at a four-alarm fire on Staten Island in 1999. In the background is Tower Ladder 77.

Adam Alberti photo

Engine 163 on Staten Island ran this 1993 Seagrave pumper with a 1,000-gpm pump and 500-gallon booster tank.

This is a similar piece that ran as Engine 165, also on Staten Island.

Adam Alberti photo

Warren Weiss photo

Engine 82 in the Bronx, named "La Casa Grande," is another 1993 Seagrave pumper and is shown working at a five-alarm fire in 1996. Note that the original bumper has been altered to increase the amount of hose that can be carried. Note also the Christmas wreath.

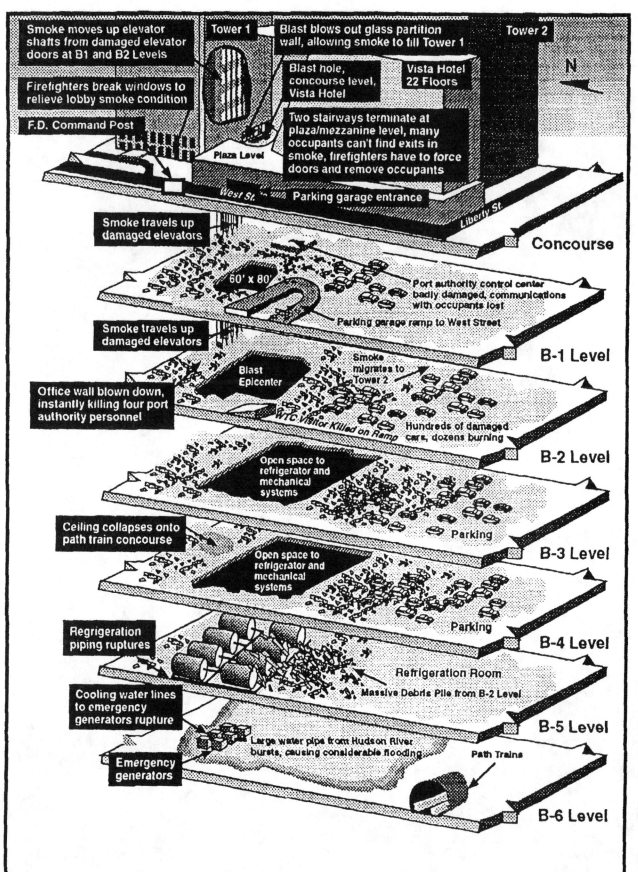

Smoke moves up elevator shafts from damaged elevator doors at B1 and B2 Levels

Firefighters break windows to relieve lobby smoke condition

F.D. Command Post

Tower 1

Blast blows out glass partition wall, allowing smoke to fill Tower 1

Tower 2

N

Blast hole, concourse level, Vista Hotel

Vista Hotel 22 Floors

Two stairways terminate at plaza/mezzanine level, many occupants can't find exits in smoke, firefighters have to force doors and remove occupants

Plaza Level

West St.   Parking garage entrance   Liberty St.

Smoke travels up damaged elevators

Concourse

60' x 80'

Port authority control center badly damaged, communications with occupants lost

Parking garage ramp to West Street

Smoke travels up damaged elevators

B-1 Level

Blast Epicenter

Smoke migrates to Tower 2

Office wall blown down, instantly killing four port authority personnel

WTC Visitor Killed on Ramp

Hundreds of damaged cars, dozens burning

B-2 Level

Open space to refrigerator and mechanical systems

Parking

Ceiling collapses onto path train concourse

B-3 Level

Open space to refrigerator and mechanical systems

Parking

Refrigeration piping ruptures

B-4 Level

Refrigeration Room

Massive Debris Pile from B-2 Level

Cooling water lines to emergency generators rupture

B-5 Level

Large water pipe from Hudson River bursts, causing considerable flooding

Path Trains

Emergency generators

B-6 Level

Federal Emergency Management Agency photo

The WTC had many levels of basements. This drawing shows the extent of the underground damage caused by the terrorist bombing in 1993.

Four tower ladders at work at a plumbing warehouse fire in Brooklyn, 1994.

Battalion 22's chief rides in this 1994 Chevrolet Suburban. There are two types of light bars on the roof plus red lights mounted at the bumper level.

Adam Alberti photo

Tower Ladder 79 was this 1994 Seagrave that carried a 75-foot Baker Aerialscope boom. The entire truck appears to extend some distance beyond the rear wheels.

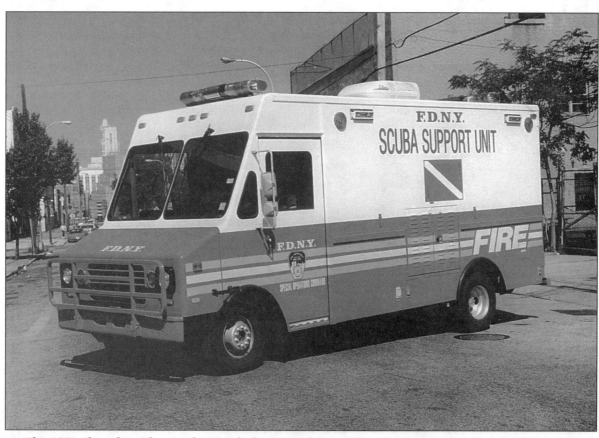

Joseph A. Pinto photo

This 1995 Chevrolet with a stand-up van body was used as a scuba support unit.

Right margin: Warren Weiss photo

Tower Ladder 54, stationed in the Bronx, used this 1995 FWD with a Saulsbury body and Baker 75-foot Aerial-scope. Note the stabilizing jack in front and outriggers to the side, and an intake hose supplying the tower. The vehicle is huge. On the front bumper is a soft-drink can.

Rescue 3, in the Bronx, ran this 1996 HME/Saulsbury.

This was a rare six-alarm blaze in 1996 at an abandoned brick commercial building at 8th Avenue and 56th Street in Manhattan.

Warren Weiss photo

A closer look at the six-alarm fire in Manhattan, 1996.

Warren Weiss photo

This was Rescue 5, a 1996 HME chassis with a Saulsbury body. It was destroyed on 9/11.

This is Engine 166, based on Staten Island. It's a 1996 Seagrave 1,000-gpm pumper with a 500-gallon booster tank.

A string of small stores in Brooklyn, 1997. The fire appears to be nearly out.

Warren Weiss photo

In pictures of newer FDNY apparatus, there are logos or emblems similar to cartoon-like pictures painted on the sides of Air Corps bombers in World War II. They were intended to develop pride in each company. This logo is used by Engine 235, in the Bedford-Stuyvesant area of Brooklyn.

Warren Weiss photo

Here is the "In the Eye of the Storm," the prophetic logo of Ladder 132, which was destroyed on 9/11.

Warren Weiss photo

Engine 246 and Ladder 169 serve a waterfront area. Their slogan is "Fightin' Brighton" and the wave of water they are carrying will engulf the burning building.

Warren Weiss photo

The symbols on Ladder 175's logo are burning multi-story buildings.

Warren Weiss photo

There must be a catchy explanation for Engine 94's logo.

Ladder 101's logo shows the "Red Hook Raiders."

FDNY's Tower Ladder 17 is this 1997 Seagrave with a 75-foot Aerialscope.

Adam Alberti photo

Joseph A. Pinto photo

This 1997 Ford flatbed carried a slip-on unit for fighting fires on the expressways.

Joseph A. Pinto photo

Note the massive brush guards protecting both the front and cab of this 1997 International used as a brush rig. Saulsbury outfitted the body.

Adam Alberti photo

This 1997 Seagrave, with a 1,000-gpm pump and 500-gallon booster tank, runs as Engine 68. Top of cab has a New York Yankees emblem and pin-striping. Engine 68 is the first company due for incidents at Yankee stadium.

Warren Weiss photo

Six one-story shops were gutted in this 1998 fire in Queens. Six firefighters were injured in a sudden backdraft.

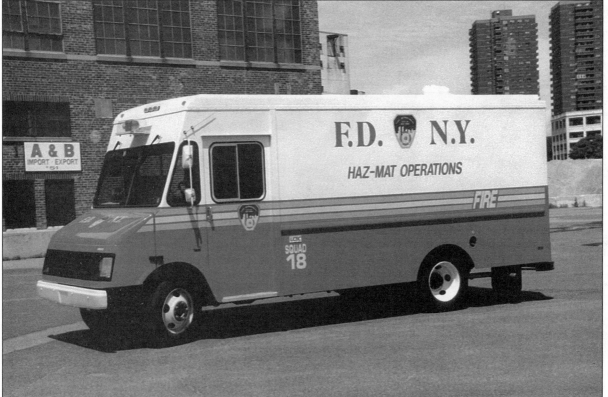

Joseph A. Pinto photo

This step van, carried on a 1998 GMC chassis, housed a hazardous materials operations truck.

Adam Alberti photo

Engine 160 is this 1998 Seagrave 1,000-gpm pumper. It also carries a 500-gallon water tank. Short lightbars on the roof are at 45-degree angles, making them more visible as the apparatus moves through intersections.

Adam Alberti photo

This 1998 Seagrave is Engine 84, based in Manhattan-Harlem. It has a 1,000-gpm pump and 500-gallon tank.

Warren Weiss photo

Tower Ladder 51, stationed in the Bronx, ran this 1998 Seagrave with a 75-foot Aerialscope. It's shown working at a four-alarm fire. Note the several extended leveling and stabilizing jacks and outriggers.

Adam Alberti photo

Squad Company 41, in the Harlem/Bronx area, ran this 1998 Seagrave 1,000-gpm pump with a 500-gallon tank. At present, "squad" companies are assigned a pumper, stocked with ladder company hand and power tools and a foam generator. They can respond as an engine company or to assist a rescue company, or to take the place of a rescue company that has responded to another call. The firefighters assigned to squad companies have extra training in dealing with chemical and biological agents, and collapse, confined space, and high-angle rescue operations.

Joseph A. Pinto photo

This 2000 Seagrave with a 1,000-gpm pump and 500-gallon tank was one of five purchased. It was assigned to Squad 61. FDNY shops added equipment boxes to carry rescue and other tools.

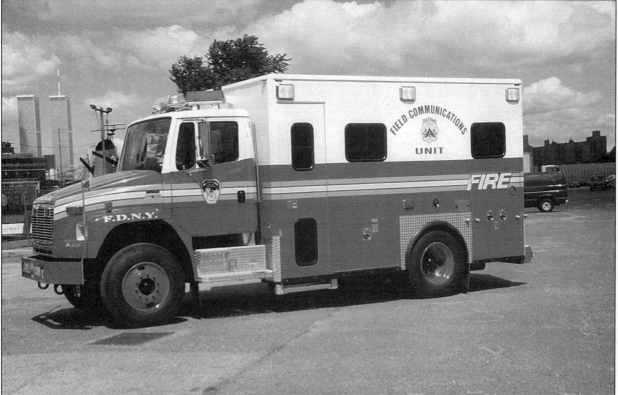

This is a field communications unit carried on a 2000 Freightliner chassis.

Manhattan's Engine 7 was this 2000 Seagrave with a 1,000-gpm pump and 500-gallon tank. It was destroyed on 9/11.

Engine 324 is this 2000 Seagrave with a 2,000-gpm pump and 500-gallon tank.

Squad 252 in Brooklyn uses this 2000 Seagrave with a 1,000-gpm pump, a 500-gallon booster tank and numerous equipment compartments.

This is Ladder 81, a 1999 Seagrave with a 100-foot rear-mount aerial, viewed from the front. License plate says "81 TRUCK."

Joseph A. Pinto photo

Ladder Company 34 received this 2000 Seagrave with a 100-foot tillered aerial.

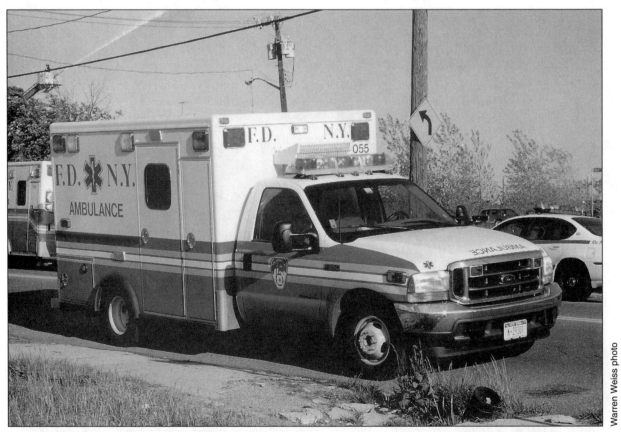

Warren Weiss photo

EMS Ambulance 55 has a McCoy Miller body on a 2000 Ford chassis. It's shown at a fire site. At top left is a hose stream from an elevated platform ladder.

This 1999 GMC Battalion Sedan is operated by FDNY's Emergency Medical Services.

Warren Weiss photo

Here's a front view of Engine 161, a 2000 Seagrave, stationed in Staten Island. Behind the bumper on left is the trash line, two 50-foot lengths of hose off a gated wye. In the center is a 4-inch front suction.

Adam Alberti photo

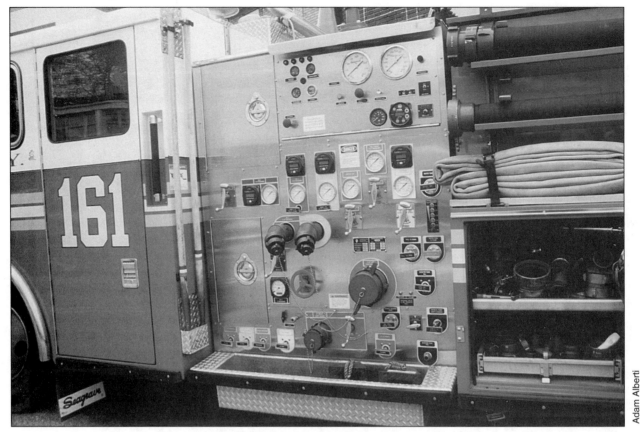

This is the pump panel on the street side. Behind the cab are pike poles.

This rear view shows a variety
of hoses, ranging from 1 3/4 to
3 inches in diameter. On the
far step is a can for collecting
biohazard waste.

Curbside view shows EMS equipment. Boards in bottom rear compartment are for CPR. Front cabinets carry extinguishers.

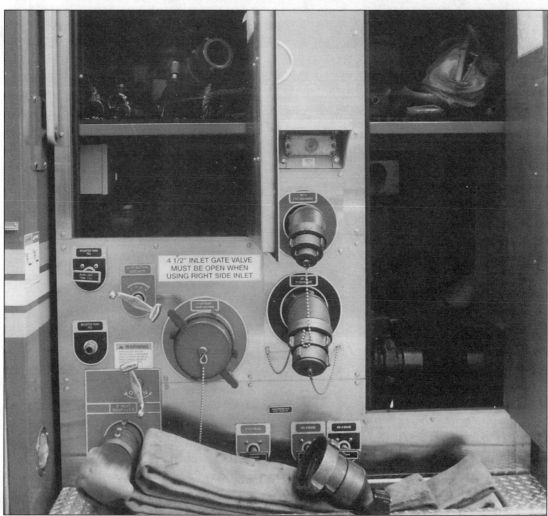

Pump panel on curbside. The 1,000-gpm pump is accessed from this side for servicing and repairs.

On driver's side are pike poles carried in a rack outside of equipment compartments. Reel of electric cord is above.

Adam Alberti photo

Adam Alberti photo

Open compartment doors on driver's side show hand tools, inflatable airbags for extrication, and a saw. Above, to right of wire reel is basket for victim removal.

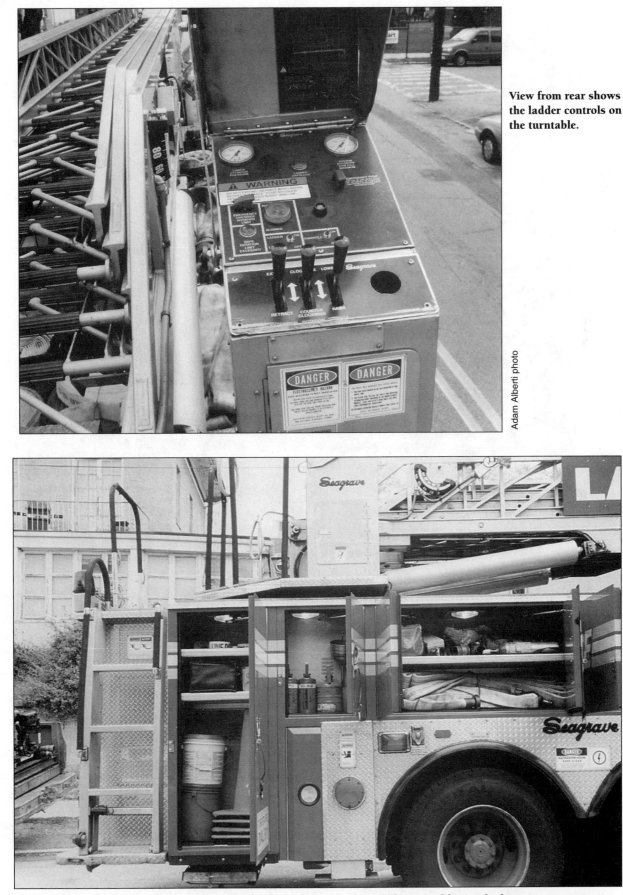

View from rear shows
the ladder controls on
the turntable.

Adam Alberti photo

Adam Alberti photo

View from curbside shows the base of the ladder and steps leading to the turntable. Inside the compartments we see orange cones, caution tape, gasoline for saws, EMS equipment, and additional hose bundles for high-rise operations. Other compartments on this side carry extraction equipment, a generator, small fire extinguishers, tools, mauls, and Indian tanks for brush fires.

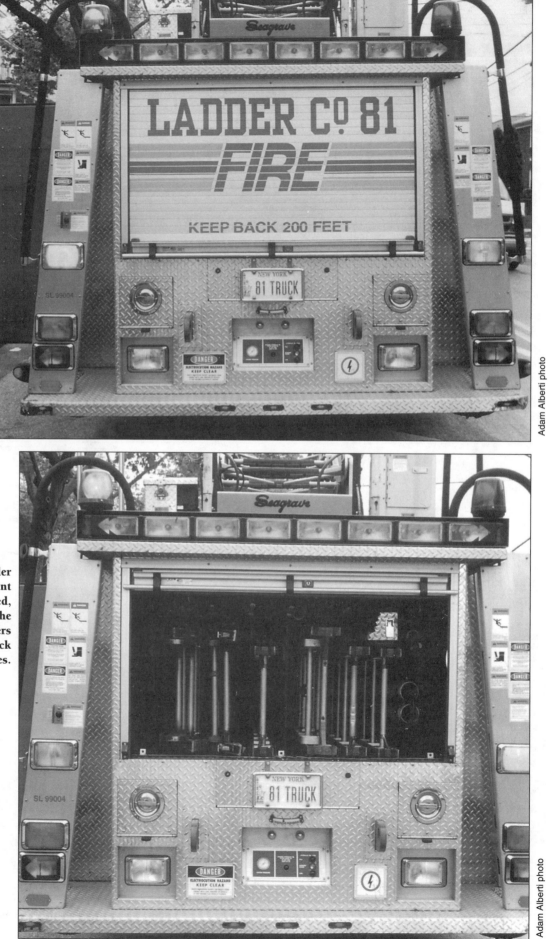

Rear view with ladder compartment door closed. How many lights can you count?

The ladder compartment door is raised, showing the ground ladders that the truck carries.

Adam Alberti photo

Adam Alberti photo

Vacant commercial property burning in a two-alarm fire in South Brooklyn, 1999.

A tower in use at a Brighton Beach fire, June, 2000.

Warren Weiss photo

Warren Weiss photo

A Harlem fire involving brownstones, 1999. Two towers are in use.

A fire in Chinatown, 1999.

Warren Weiss photo

Chapter 12

The Early 20th Century

We were hardly into the 21st century when FDNY suffered its greatest tragedy: the 9/11 destruction of the World Trade Center's twin towers. As this book was being written, the site of the WTC was still being cleared of wreckage and bodies of less than half of the missing firefighters had been recovered. For U.S. citizens who are of the writers' generation, Pearl Harbor was a defining moment of our lifetime. For Americans who are younger, 9/11 may be a similar, horrific benchmark.

Much of the story has yet to be told. This book deals with apparatus, and we shall attempt to focus on that subject, and hope that we do not appear to ignoring the terrible toll of lives lost. From the viewpoint of an apparatus historian, it seems certain that 9/11 set a record for one-time loss of apparatus at the scene of a disaster.

At the time of 9/11 FDNY was operating 211 engine companies (including seven as squads) plus 143 ladder companies. Considerable apparatus was involved in the WTC disaster. Elizabeth Kolbert

Warren Weiss photo

This 2001 American LaFrance Eagle has a 1,000-gpm pump and 500-gallon tank, and was assigned to Engine 34 to replace a destroyed Seagrave, that was lost on 9/11. Note roll-up equipment compartment doors. The truck had been delivered to FDNY as a demonstrator prior to 9/11 and it was to have been tested and evaluated. After 9/11, FDNY decided to place it into service.

wrote in the *New Yorker*: "The first and second alarms, whichwere transmitted together, sounded at 8:47 a.m., the third at 8:50. At 8:55 a 10-60 went out, signaling a major emergency, and four minutes later a fifth alarm sounded ... (FDNY) has no formal designation for a blaze that requires more than five alarms, but on September 11 the there were five for the north tower and five for the south tower, and still the alarms continued to ring, first in fire houses in Chelsea and Chinatown, and then in Brooklyn Heights and Williamsburg, and then all across the city, so that in less than 30 minutes more than a hundred companies had been called out. Ladder 24 was called from midtown, and Engine 214 from Bedford-Stuyvesant, and so was Squad 288 from Maspeth, Queens and Ladder 105 from downtown Brooklyn. Even after the two towers collapsed and tens of thousands or people came streaming out of lower Manhattan covered with ash, the firemen kept coming."[1]

The disaster is etched in most Americans' minds. As this book is being written the death toll is estimated at just under 3,000. Included in this figure are 347 firefighters, 37 Port Authority Officers, 12 EMT and paramedics, three New York City court officers, 23 New York City police officers, one FBI officer and one U.S. Secret Service officer.[2] In the U.S., there is no comparable loss of life for public safety workers. In 1947, 27 volunteers were killed in a Texas City blast involving on a French freighter. FDNY, upon until 9/11/01, had lost 752 people in the previous127 years. The 9/11 disaster hit some companies especially hard. Rescue 1, which had lost four members between 1925 and 1995, lost 11 men on 9/11.

The insurance company-sponsored New York Fire Patrol had its three trucks at the WTC site and two of its members were injured and one is missing. Its Unit 2, a 1999 GMC/Ferrara, was destroyed, but will be replaced.

Considerable FDNY apparatus was destroyed and damaged. There is no other comparable loss of equipment in U. S. firefighting history. One tally of 9/11 losses, released on October 19, 2001, by FDNY listed:19 pumpers, 18 ladder and tower ladders, two rescues, one tactical rescue support unit, one satellite wagon, one mask service unit, two support units, two fleet maintenance trucks, 10 ambulances, 24 sedans, and 16 GMC Suburbans.[3] Other equipment was damaged.

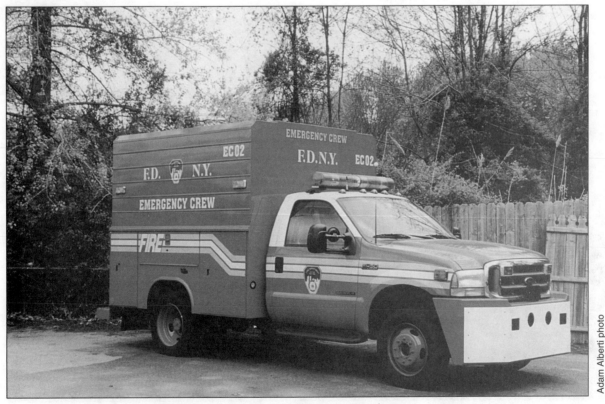

A 2001 Ford F450 with a Reading body used by an FDNY emergency crew.

Adam Alberti photo

1. Elizabeth Kolbert, "The Chief," *The New Yorker* (October 8, 2001), p. 42.

2. Wysiwyg://148/http://www.publicsafe.net/fdny_main.htm (March 19, 2002).

3. "Up From the Ashes, FDNY Rebuilds," *Fire Apparatus*, November/December 2001, p. 4. Slightly different numbers are reported elsewhere, the changes may occur in determining what should be salvaged.

In FDNY's shops 200 people worked 12-hour shifts cleaning and repairing serviceable units and stripping usable equipment from those rigs that were to be scrapped. Some 80 pieces of FDNY apparatus were removed from the WTC scene, cleaned, repaired, tested and placed back into service within four days of the incident.[4] Workers in the FDNY shops were aided by personnel from Seagrave and Saulsbury factories and dealerships. (Seagrave and Saulsbury are currently FDNY's major apparatus suppliers.) The two firms also contacted other customers for whom they were completing apparatus and asked whether they could send the nearly completed trucks to New York City first if they were needed. Their customers agreed.

At the time of 9/11, FDNY had three stores of reserve apparatus it could draw upon immediately. It had 20 pumpers in a reserve fleet that were already stocked with hose and with loose equipment such as nozzles and breathing apparatus kept in boxes sealed with a steel band that the officer in charge could cut. Engines in this fleet are serviced and maintained to the same standards as first-line apparatus. They are intended for use in case of civil unrest or a high incidence of alarms, such as may occur on a Fourth of July.

The second source of reserve apparatus was "spares." About 10 percent of the first-line fleet was being repaired or tested or otherwise inactive. Most were to be found at FDNY shops. After 9/11 they were immediately restocked with hose and other equipment and sent to serve in individual stations. Many retired personnel showed up at FDNY's shops to help restock this apparatus so that it could be put back into service. The third source of replacement apparatus was 10 pumpers and five ladder trucks that were assigned to the training operation.[5]

On October 25, 2001, FDNY placed an order with Seagrave for 17 rear-mount aerials, five tillered ladders, five tower ladders and one cab/chassis to rebody a damaged tower ladder. It also ordered 26 engines, including four high-pressure models, three squads and 19 standard pumpers. From Saulsbury, it ordered five rescue vehicles with walk-in bodies and dual rear axles, two tactical support bodies on International chassis, two high-rise units (used for fighting fires far above the ground) on Mack chassis, and one satellite

Three Queens Tower Ladders battle a four-alarm blaze that began in an all-night supermarket in May, 2001. Fires involving a row of stores are often multiple-alarm and sometimes referred to as "taxpayers' fires." Tower Ladder 138 is the closest. On the most distant tower are painted the words: "Rise to the Occasion."

Warren Weiss photo

4. Ibid.

5. Ibid.

hose wagon on a Mack chassis. FDNY also ordered smaller support trucks, GMC Suburbans, Ford Excursions and Ford Crown Victoria autos. The federal government, through a grant from FEMA (Federal Emergency Management Agency), is paying for a portion of the costs of replacing the FDNY apparatus.

Donated equipment included a Ferrera pumper, a Spartan Ladder Tower, a Kenworth/Pierce air and light unit, a Freightliner/E-One with a box body, and a Luverne pumper. Other donations are expected to follow. For example a Web site for the "Spirit of Oklahoma Challenge" indicated that, as of March 18, 2002, $117,000 had been collected toward buying a replacement apparatus for FDNY. (In 1995, after the bombing of the federal office building in Oklahoma City, several FDNY personnel had gone to Oklahoma to assist and, subsequently some of these same people were killed on 9/11.[6])

Countless people throughout the world donated money to assist the survivors of 9/11. Many of communities throughout the United States raised money to buy new fire apparatus to replace what FDNY lost in the disaster. For example, Akron, Ohio, raised about $1.4 million dollars to purchase a new Seagrave tower ladder. The fund drive there had been spirited by a columnist for the *Akron Beacon Journal*.

A bronze plaque on the side of the truck says: "A Gift from the People of Greater Akron." The truck has been assigned to be Ladder 163, in the Queens. The amount raised in Akron was large enough that it was also used to purchase two ambulances and three police cruisers lost on 9/11. Another major fund-raising drive was being conducted in South Carolina where, more than 100 years ago, some apparatus was received from New York City to replace some local equipment that had been destroyed.

In Clintonville, Wisconsin, Seagrave announced that it would donate a complete pumper to FDNY. Employees of Seagrave designed and donated American flag graphics that appeared on both sides of a 100-foot rear-mount aerial ladder truck delivered to FDNY. E-One, an apparatus builder located in Ocala, Florida, donated a rescue truck that will be used as a decontamination unit.

A Saulsbury rescue truck was given by Airbus, the European aircraft. Pierce Manufacturing, Inc., of Appleton, Wisconsin, donated an air and light support rescue truck, built on a Kenworth chassis.

The events of 9/11 were a major blow to the nation, New York City and NYFD. All are on their way to recovery.

Warren Weiss photo

Firemen fight fires; fire engines only help. Here we see firemen at work in the Queens on October 6, 2001. This four-alarm blaze was New York's first major fire following 9/11.

6. http://www.spiritofoklahoma.org (March 19. 2002).

Seagrave Tower Ladder 135 at a furniture warehouse fire in the Queens in October 2001. Just to the left of the extended ladder is a waterway leading up to platform. Other extended ladders and platforms are visible in the distance.

Warren Weiss

After 9/11, FDNY was also short of small trucks used to support and supply the department. Reading Body Works, of Shillington, Pennsylvania, received a contract to build, install, and paint 55 custom bodies for FDNY. The trucks had dual rear wheels. Features included "automotive-quality rotary locks for secure protection to tools and equipment; stainless steel bolt-on hinges keeping the compartment doors operating smoothly in all weather conditions; and double-paneled compartment doors offering greater durability."

Ladder 128, in the Queens, uses this 2001 Seagrave 100-foot rear-mount aerial.

Adam Alberti photo

Tower Ladder 152, stationed in Queens, operates this 2001 Seagrave with a 95-foot Baker Aerialscope.

Joseph A. Pinto photo

This 2001 Seagrave was assigned to Engine 6. It had a 1,000-gpm pump and carried 500 gallons of water.

Ladder 49's rear-mount aerial was built by Seagrave in 2001.

Joseph A. Pinto photo

This 2001 Seagrave has a rear-mount aerial ladder and ran as Ladder No. 11.

Adam Alberti photo

This 2001 Spartan Gladiator was a demonstrator used by FDNY. It had a 75-foot Baker boom and ran as Tower Ladder 105 in Brooklyn.

Warren Weiss photo

In New York, there were many displays of grief and pride following the losses of life on 9/11. This Brooklyn citizen's Christmas-time display thanks New York City's fire, police, and EMS services.

Brush Fire Unit 4 serves on Staten Island. It uses a 2002 Ford F450 with a Knapheide body.

Rear view shows pump and hose. The rig carries 150 feet of 2 1/2-inch hose, 250 feet of 1 3/4-inch hose, 500 feet of 1-inch hose, plus booster hose on a Hannay reel.

A 2002 International carrying a Saulsbury body and used to carry Tactical Support unit 2. It's equipped with an array of lighting, a boat, an outboard motor and a small crane.

This is a 2002 Ferrara Inferno with a 1,000-gpm pump and 500-gallon tank, serving as Engine 283 in Brooklyn. The pump was a gift to New York City from the people of Louisiana who responded to a fund-raising drive led by Louisiana Gov. M. J. "Mike" Foster, Jr.

Luverne Fire Apparatus, of Brandon, South Dakota, a subsidiary of Spartan Motors, built and donated this pumper, with a 1,000-gpm Darley pump, to FDNY after the 9/11 disaster. The fire engine was a gift of the two firms, their employees, and their venders. The Luverne firm was originally in Minnesota.

Luverne Fire Apparatus photo

This is a 2002 Seagrave rear-mount aerial built for FDNY. Employees of Seagrave paid for the American flag design.

This new logo/mural is carried on Squad Engine 288. It shows the WTC towers and lists 19 firefighters who were lost.

Seagrave employees in early 2002 in front of three pieces of apparatus on their way to FDNY. The vehicle on the left is lettered Squad Co, 1. A rear-mount aerial is in the center and a pumper on the right.

Brett Romberg, Seagrave photo

Pump controls on a 2002 Seagrave pumper being completed for FDNY.

Brett Romberg, Seagrave photo

Rear view of a pumper destined for New York. At top right we see a ground ladder.

This medallion is placed on each piece of Seagrave apparatus headed for FDNY.

Brett Romberg, Seagrave photo

Mike Luckovich, of the *Atlanta Constitution*, drew this poignant cartoon that appeared shortly after 9/11. Reproduced with permission of Mike Luckovich and Creators Syndicate, Inc.

Bibliography

Ahrens-Fox Bulletins 156,159, circa-1925.

American City, The, various issues 1915-1965.

Calderone, John A., *The History of Fire Engines* (Greenwich, CT: Brompton, 1997).

--------- and Jack Lerch, Wheels of the Bravest: A History of FDNY Fire Apparatus, 1865-1982, (Howard Beach, New York, Fire Apparatus Journal Publications, 1984).

Fusco, Anthony L., "Report from Chief of Department," in *The World Trade Center Bombing Report and Analysis* (Washington. D.C.: Federal Emergency Management Agency, ca. 1994) pp. 1-21.

http://home.earthlink.net/~efdff/WEB22_fdny_firehistory.html (January 30, 2002).

http://members.aol.com/fdnyemswebsite/ (January 30, 2002).

http://www.code3.net/c3asp/search.asp (January 23, 2002).

http://www.gov.state.la.us/press/buckforfiretruck.htm (March19, 2002).

http://www.nycfiremuseum.org/History/hist11.html (December 5, 2001).

http://www.nycfiremuseum.org/newsletter/curators.htm (December 5, 2001).

http://www.rescue1fdny.com/comhistory.html (March 19, 2002).

http://www.spiritofoklahoma.org (March 19. 2002).

http://chiefsaide.tripod.com/fdnybeginnersguide/id9.html (March 18, 2002).

Johnson, Gus, *F.D.N.Y, The Fire Buff's Handbook of the New York Fire Department 1900-1975* (Belmont, Massachusetts: Western Islands, 1977).

Kandell, Jonathan, "Boss," *Smithsonian*, February, 2002, pp. 84-90.

Kolbert, Elizabeth, "The Chief," *The New Yorker*, October 8, 2001, pp. 42-47.

Lee, Mathew, *A Pictorial History of the Fire Engine, Volume 2, The decade of the 1920s* (Plymouth, Michigan: the author, 1999).

Limpus, Lowell M., *History of the New York Fire Department* (New York: E. P. Dutton, 1940).

"Louisiana Gives FDNY a Gift from the Heart: A New Pumper," *Fire Apparatus*, February, 2002, pp. 1 and 7.

McCall, Walter P., *American Fire Engines Since 1900* (Glen Ellyn, Illinois: Crestline, 1976).

Phillips, Lawrence E. *American LaFrance 700 Series 1945-1952 Photo Archive, Volume 2* (Hudson, Wisconsin: Iconografix, 2000).

----------, *American LaFrance 700 & 800 Series 1953-1958 Photo Archive,* (Hudson, Wisconsin: Iconografix, 1999).

"Up From the Ashes, FDNY Rebuilds," *Fire Apparatus*, November/December 2001, pp. 1-8.

Wagner, Rob Leicester, *Fire Engines* (New York: MetroBooks, 1996).

Wohleber, Curt, "The Fire Hydrant," *Invention & Technology*, Winter 2002, pp.10-11.

Wood, Donald F. and Wayne Sorensen, *Big City Fire Trucks*, Volume 1, 1900-1950 (Iola, Wisconsin: Krause, 1996).

---------, *Big City Fire Trucks*, Volume 2, 1951-1996 (Iola, Wisconsin: Krause, 1997).

"World Center Tragedy," *Tow Times*, November, 2001, pp. 30-33.

Wysiwyg://148/http://www.publicsafe.net/fdny_main.htm (March 19, 2002).

INDEX BY MANUFACTURER

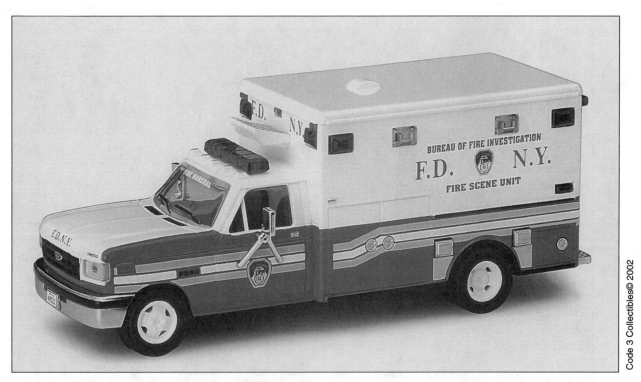

Code 3 Collectibles© 2002

Code 3 Collectibles makes 1/64 replicas of fire apparatus. Here is their model showing a Ford F-350 with body and markings as would be used by an FDNY fire marshal.

Code 3 Collectibles© 2002

This is a kit offered by Code 3 that includes a battalion consisting of an aerial ladder, a pumper, a rescue squad and a chief's car.

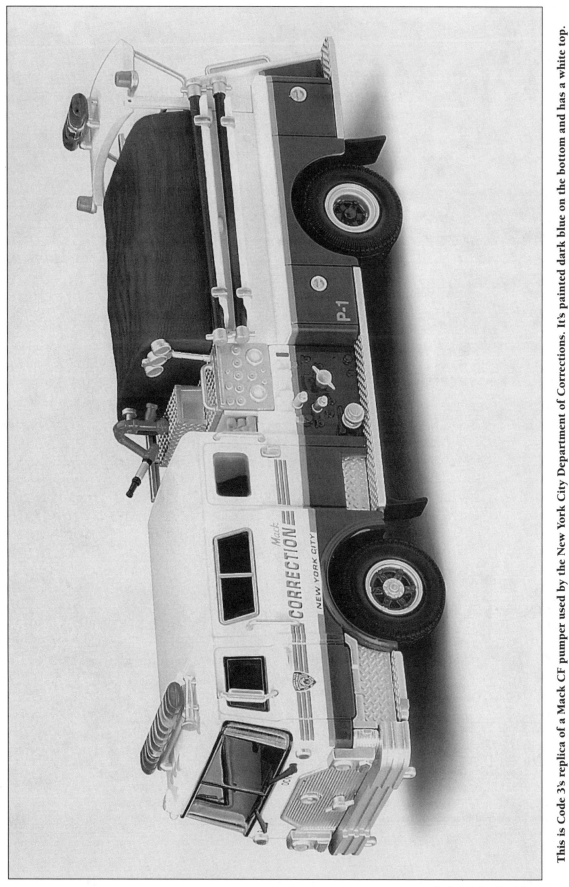

This is Code 3's replica of a Mack CF pumper used by the New York City Department of Corrections. It's painted dark blue on the bottom and has a white top.

About The Authors

Wayne Sorensen is a professor emeritus at San Jose State University, and Donald F. Wood is a professor at San Francisco State University. They have co-authored six books about fire apparatus, including three others published by Krause that are still in print, *Volunteer Fire Trucks, Big City Fire Trucks I* and *Big City Fire Trucks II*.

Sorensen belongs to the Fire Associates of Santa Clara County, the Society for the Preservation and Appreciation of Antique Fire Appartus in America, and the Sacramento Fire Buff Club. Wood belongs to the American Truck Historical Society, the Society of Automotive Historians, and is on the Advisory Board of the Hays Antique Truck Museum in Woodland, California.

Wayne Sorensen   **Donald F. Wood**

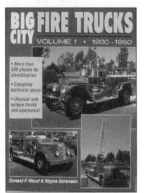
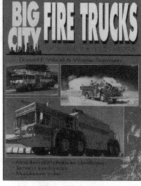
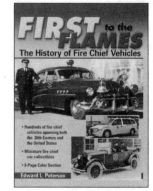
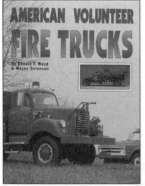
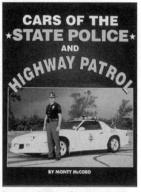